FINISHING
TOUCHES

FINISHING
TOUCHES

ELIZABETH HILLIARD

CROWN PUBLISHERS, INC.

NEW YORK

Edited and designed by Conran Octopus Limited
37 Shelton Street
London WC2H 9HN

Project Editor: Jackie Matthews
Copy Editor: Elizabeth Haldane
Art Director: Mary Evans
Design: The Image
Picture Researcher: Jessica Walton
Illustrator: Cherrill Parris
Production: Jackie Kernaghan
Editorial Assistant: Helen Ridge

Published by Crown Publishers, Inc.
201 East 50th Street
New York, New York 10022.
Member of the Crown Publishing Group.

Originally published in Great Britain by
Conran Octopus Limited in 1990

CROWN is a registered trademark of
Crown Publishers, Inc.

Manufactured in Singapore

Library of Congress Cataloging-in-Publication
Data available upon request.

ISBN 0-517-58316-X

10 9 8 7 6 5 4 3 2 1

First American Edition

Where terminology differs, the British word is
followed by the American equivalent in brackets.

CONTENTS

INTRODUCTION

There comes a point in the decoration of a home when you have to adjust your focus from the big things to the little ones. The grand schemes like structural alterations and the colour of the walls are complete, but the rooms seem very far from finished. What is wanted is character and that lived-in look which will be created by your choice of curtains and carpets, upholstery and lighting, and the way you arrange and display your pictures and possessions. We have all visited houses and apartments that are nothing more than cold, featureless shells which are 'not quite right', and other homes that overflow with the personality of the owner. Whether the inhabitants of these homes are sophisticated and elegant or hale and hearty, whether they live in the centre of the city or the depths of rolling country, the rooms of their homes are welcoming and interesting.

Some people simply have the gift of knowing where to put what and can instinctively organize colour, pattern and space. But for most of us it is a question of looking about and gradually picking up tips and ideas. In this way we slowly learn to make the most of our home and the things we put in its rooms and build up an individual style. One way to begin is with a little detective work. The period of your home and your furniture will offer a lead, which you can have fun following up by looking at preserved and restored houses of the same period and by studying paintings and prints of contemporary interiors. The purpose of such research is not to imitate historic interiors but to develop a style relevant to you, your home and your way of life, with sufficient historical resonance to prevent it becoming dated. The past, in other words, has a lively and significant contribution to make to your future surroundings.

This book is an essential source of inspiration for all those aspects of decorating that come after the plasterer, plumber and painter have finished their tasks. Designed to help take the hard work out of creating a style, its text and pictures together offer a rich collection of practical suggestions, many of which are very simple, for everything from pelmet (window cornice) designs to the arrangement of pots and pans in the kitchen. There are ideas for adding interest to all the structural parts of a room: doors and windows, walls, ceilings and floors; for making the most of fireplaces and dealing with radiators; for choosing fabric and an appropriate design for curtains, loose covers, cushions and beds. Lighting can make all the difference to the atmosphere of a room and the range of light fittings has never been greater. Central lighting and other important lighting problems are discussed and stimulating solutions provided. The hanging of pictures and display of objects and collections of every kind can give life to a room, as will the clever use of fresh, dried and even artificial flowers and foliage. Rooms designed purely for practical use, like the kitchen and bathroom, can be transformed with arrangements of cooking equipment and storage jars or soaps and towels.

Ideas from the most inviting and original homes in many countries are here gathered together in one book. You may have moved house, you may have altered or extended your rooms, or you may simply feel like a change but not want to undertake extensive and expensive redecoration. The following pages are brimming over with advice on how to give character, cohesion and warmth to the appearance of your home.

Left: *Before photography became universal, the only way to preserve accurate records of many birds and animals was to stuff them. These fine examples, protected by glass cases, make a handsome display on open shelving. Some of the shelves are backed with mirror glass.*
Right: *A sofa loaded with cushions is rich in colour and pattern.*

WALLS

'You have yellow walls – so have I; yellow
is the colour of joy.'

Oscar Wilde

Left: *Elegant
panelling and dado
(wainscoting) have
been conjured from
a plain wall with
paint above and
below a real chair
rail. The wall rises
in shades of golden
yellow, its panels
edged with wide
lines mitred at the
corners, above the
horizontal stone-
coloured dado.*
Right: *Stucco relief
is cleverly imitated
in delicate browns,
greys and white on
buff background.*

Walls are what make a room. They define its size and proportions and act as a vast backdrop for everything that is in the room at the same time as being its most dominant element. When you walk into a hallway or drawing room you have never seen before, the first thing you notice may be a piece of furniture or an object. The atmosphere and character of the room, however, will have been created by the colour of the walls and the way they are decorated. If you removed all but the most basic contents from the room, the atmosphere would remain, but if you left the contents and replaced the walls, the mood of the room would change appreciably. This is largely because of the power of colour, which is more immediately visible on the walls than anywhere else. The combined area of walls is generally greater than the surface area of any other element in the room such as ceiling, floor or windows.

By the finishing touches stage the colour of the walls will probably have been decided and they will have been decorated. Even now, however, it is ▶

possible to alter greatly the appearance of your walls by measures such as highlighting architectural details, adding borders and repainting or papering limited areas in order to improve the appearance of the whole room. An extra, textured, layer of colour can be added by rag-rolling or sponging it over the existing colour. Clever use of mirrors can transform a room and, perhaps most import- ant of all, so can your choice of pictures and other wall hangings and the way you organize them, not only in each room but in vistas from one room to another and in passages.

In their undecorated state walls will vary hugely according to the size, age and style of the house and the extent to which they have escaped alteration since the house was built. In eighteenth- and nineteenth-century houses the walls are often enlivened by decorative architectural features such as coving, cor- nices (crown moldings), friezes, picture rails, chair rails, dados (wainscoting) and skirting boards (baseboards). In a twentieth-century modernist home the aim of the architect was to sweep away the past and create, in the words of the architect Le Corbusier, a 'machine for living in'. Walls in such a house are smooth and sheer, unadorned with the architectural details used in previous centuries for practical purposes and to break up the monotony of plain walls. It would be inappropriate to apply any of these details to walls intended to be free of them. However, where such architec- tural features already exist, they provide an unequalled opportunity to create a rich and in- teresting interior and so should be treated with respect and given some attention. In houses that have suffered severe 'modernization' or have lost such features they can be restored, though this may prove costly. It may be more practical to devise surface decoration that in- corporates or develops the invisible lines left by vanished architectural detailing.

Borders give walls definition and a sense of importance. The uppermost architectural bor- der on a wall is the cornice (crown molding), a projecting ornamental moulding at the join with the ceiling. For a long time the cornice was considered an essential feature – one nineteenth-century architectural commenta- tor said 'Without a cornice, no room can have a finished appearance'. If a cornice has been painted repeatedly over the years, the detail may have become clogged with old paint but will come to life again if cleaned. The opera- tion requires some delicacy to avoid dam- aging the moulding, which will be made either

of plaster or papier mâché unless the house is very old and the walls are panelled, in which case it may be made of wood.

The results of cleaning can be stunning. A cornice that looked lumpen and uninteresting will spring sharply into focus, revealing details like scrolls and curled leaves that were not visible before. Once clean, the cornice can be painted in various ways. The colour of the ceiling can be continued down over it, though this will encourage it to blend in with the ceiling rather than stand out against it. Alternatively, a colour found elsewhere on the wall can be used, such as a background colour from the wallpaper or the frieze, or another colour that complements those already chosen. The cornice's three-dimensional qualities will be

Above: *Gluing engravings to the walls in artistic patterns was an 18th-century ladies' amusement. Today, photocopies washed with tea and edged with printed borders can give the same impressive effect.*

Opposite top: *Daring use of strong colour draws attention to the demarcation of walls and ceiling. Shades of terracotta and mustard link flat areas, with architectural elements in cooler blue and green. China figurines provide a three-dimensional frieze.*

Opposite bottom: *In a dining room enriched with Etruscan colours, the dado is marbled and wall panels are decorated with scenes from classical mythology.*

emphasized if it is painted in a combination of colours or shades with a lighter one on the more prominent parts. Simple cornices made from continuous plain moulding can be effectively treated in a similar manner.

Below the cornice is the area known as the frieze, which in most nineteenth-century houses is defined at its bottom edge by a moulded wooden picture rail. In classical architecture the frieze was a flat area in the entablature between the cornice above and the architrave below. Architects and artists used this for decorative reliefs depicting men, gods and animals enacting heroic deeds and mythological scenes. The Parthenon, where the frieze shows a procession honouring the goddess Athena, is the most famous and

Opposite: Delft tiles were used as damp-proofing in 17th- and 18th-century Dutch houses. Panels showing flowers and animals are here surrounded by witjes *– plain white tiles of many shades.*

Right: The structure of painted panelling with its repeated verticals is emphasized by stencilled borders, with areas between punctuated by stencilled flowers and curly geometric motifs, all in gentle colours.

spectacular surviving example of this. To make the most of the humble, domestic frieze today you need to kindle an attitude similar to that of the ancients, by looking at it as an opportunity not to be lost rather than a problem. The possibilities are enormous.

If you have a spark of artistic talent or simply fancy having a go with a paintbrush, the most original option for the frieze is to decorate it yourself, painting freehand with one or more colours. It is not necessary to plan a detailed and complicated design – a few rough ideas sketched on paper first will act as a guide, and a soft pencil or piece of chalk can be used to make outlines on the wall if this is necessary. A pattern of bold geometric shapes is probably the easiest to draw, followed by a design of scrolls and swirls. You can give your frieze decoration a basic structure by first cutting out some cardboard shapes of the main elements of the design and drawing around these on the wall. Figurative frieze designs traditionally tell a story, so yours could tell the story of your life or a favourite childhood story or mythological scene. The execution does not have to be highly finished and professional – indeed it will probably have more impact if it is not. A great many people are convinced they cannot draw and paint and are frightened of making fools of themselves if they try. Painting a frieze is quite simple and the rewards are greater than the dangers. If you are not happy with the results, you can paint over it.

An alternative to doing it yourself is to commission an artist or muralist to paint one for you. It can be painted on removable panels so that you can take your investment with you if you move house (you can, of course, do the same if you paint the frieze yourself – it will save you having to spend so much time up a step-ladder). Less expensive alternatives to a specially commissioned frieze include photocopying a frieze or stencilling it. Many libraries have pattern books of frieze designs from the eighteenth and nineteenth centuries. A photocopy of one of these (or any other design that is out of copyright) can be enlarged, repeated, and pasted on the walls having perhaps been coloured first (it can also be photocopied on coloured paper). Stencils can be bought or made and are a quick method of reproducing attractively fresh patterns *ad infinitum*. If you make your own stencils and the walls below the frieze are papered, choose a motif from the pattern and develop it, perhaps enlarging and simplifying it. You could also repeat the design down the sides of the doors and windows.

Below the frieze the wall falls away to the skirting board (baseboard) at floor level, and sometimes has a chair rail and dado (wainscoting) at waist height or higher. A wall that has all these features is a playground for the creatively minded decorator. Each part of the wall can be decorated differently with the main belt of colour and interest being between waist height and the picture rail. With all its parts planned together as a whole in terms of colour and pattern, this sort of scheme can look marvellously rich and varied. Wallpaper can be used in a cost-effective way, since it need only be hung on the main part of the walls, which may mean that a well-designed, better quality paper can be chosen. If you have not already painted the walls, consider using a stronger or deeper colour than you would usually choose, especially in a fairly dark room. The frieze and dado will prevent the effect being overbearing, and the room will seem warmer. No dark room is successfully transformed into a light one by being painted a pale colour – the result is only an unwelcoming coldness.

The dado can be decorated so that it picks up a colour from the wallpaper – ideally a fairly bold contrast in terms of light and dark, but not something so bright that it will compete with the main wall. Alternatively, it can be painted to contrast with or complement the wall colour. A dado painted plain white beneath a brilliant green wall looks fresh and strong, but may not

be practical in a house with dogs or small children, whereas a grey dado beneath a predominantly mustard or terracotta paper is more mellow and restrained. Two other treatments – ones favoured by the Victorians – are either to cover the dado with sheets of marbled paper, which are then varnished for protection, or else to cover it with anaglypta paper (relief wallpaper), before painting it an appropriate deep or strong colour.

If the skirting (baseboard), chair rail, picture rail and even cornice are all painted the same colour, or with the same decorative finish, their repeated horizontals will be emphasized and will create a satisfying visual rhythm. Alternatively, particular features can

Above: *Dynamic contrasts are created by black-and-white pictures, floor and* trompe l'œil *balustrade against egg-yolk yellow walls finished with a border at the top. A jagged pelmet dramatizes the window.*

Opposite: *Paper borders need not be confined to tops of walls – here the border runs down corners, doors and above the skirting. The* trompe l'œil *curtain has been painted to look as if it has been drawn to one side.*

be linked together by giving them similar treatment: the skirting and the cornice can be given the same decorative finish like marb-

ling, or the skirting and the chair rail painted in the same colour, which is then continued around the door surround. Drawing and colouring rough pictures of the different alternatives will give you an indication of the final appearance of the wall and may make it easier to reach a decision.

Skirting protects the bottom of the wall and prevents furniture from rubbing against the wall higher up. It tends to suffer a certain amount of wear and tear so it needs to be painted with a tough finish. In recent decades it has been usual to paint skirting white, but this is not necessarily the most practical colour and any other will do – a dark colour will not show scuff marks so readily. Stained bare

wood or wood-grained skirting is practical as is skirting covered with black, brown or grey gloss paint. However, decorative consider-ations will probably be more important than practical ones, and whatever colour is chosen it should complement the main wall colour, and in most schemes it should be continued up around the door jamb.

Not everyone is lucky enough to have walls enlivened by architectural detailing. But this way of dividing up the wall can be used as an outline guide for the creative decoration of a dull flat wall that needs definition and decora-tion. Borders can be added along the top of the walls and down the corners where walls meet. A border can be a plain painted line, or a patterned paper strip of the type now made in various widths by wallpaper manufacturers. The colours and designs of these borders often echo the pattern of wallpapers made by the same company and vary from rich and elaborate designs to fine and delicate ones. In a small but tall room, a painted or paper bor-der can be applied towards the top of the walls, about 30 cm (12 in) or more down from the ceiling, so that the proportions feel more comfortable. A decorative border can also be added at chair-rail height around the room to help break up the wall further.

Walls outlined with a band of colour 15- 20 cm (6–8 in) in from each edge, either to the floor or to chair-rail height, will spring to life. The subtlest choice of colour for them is a darker or lighter shade of the same colour as the walls, or a contrasting colour that appears elsewhere in the room, in the soft furnishings, for example. In a more ambitious scheme the horizontals of this band can be painted a dif-ferent shade to the verticals and mitred at the corners. The corners can also be indented, either with a simple right-angle or with a motif that links the walls to other details in the room — a fleur-de-lis, for example, or a star shape that may appear on curtain or furnishing fabric.

By picking motifs such as these, entire walls can be drawn into a decorative scheme that previously seemed cold and remote. If the curtain fabric shows cornucopia overflowing with fruit, for example, the shape of the cornu-copia or a piece of the fruit can be drawn out and a stencil made from it. Mix a semi-transparent colour slightly lighter or darker than the colour of the walls and pounce the cornucopia shape through the stencil in a regu-lar or random pattern across the walls. The result will be the transformation of flat colour into areas of movement and depth. The shape

Below: *A room without any architectural detailing can be enlivened if one wall is painted a different colour to the others.*

Bottom left: *Rough-plastered walls painted white and hung with gilt-framed pictures create a rich but airy effect.*

Right: *The surface of this subtle grey wall has gained movement and interest by the addition of narrow strips of wood.*

Bottom right: *A frieze and bookcases have been decorated with rampant patterns on an Egyptian theme.*

should be a fairly simple and bold one, both to limit the amount of work involved and to prevent the walls from appearing fussy. In a child's bedroom a series of bold outline shapes such as stars, moons, letters and numbers, knives and forks, and animals and birds applied in this way will make the walls interesting and stimulating.

MIRRORS

Mirrors are well known for providing additional light and a sense of space, but they can be used also to create illusion and interest in interiors. They can be divided into those that are attached to walls (or doors), and those that are framed and hung on walls amongst pictures and other decorations. Mirror that is attached can be used either as a screen to conceal or

Above left: *A framed mirror on the wall and matching mirror-topped console table reflect light on to bare dusty pink walls. The form and material of the fine wrought-iron staircase balustrade, seen deliberately reflected in the mirror, inspired the mirror frame and console.*

Above right: *Clever use of an angled mirror panel and triangular display shelf in a stark modern interior creates a new vista and 'invisible' storage space.*

Opposite: *A circular stairwell dictates that the neighbouring room has a partly rounded wall which here has been lined with smooth wooden batons which accentuate the wall's sensuously rippling curve.*

purely as a method of making space seem greater than it is. Cupboards covered with mirror will disappear, whereas dark and narrow spaces will appear to double in size. Mirrored glass is made in many colours and the selection of the right tint can assist in the creation of an illusion. A dark passage with walls painted smoky blue could have bluish mirror attached along the length of one wall. A blank passage wall opposite the door to a room can be dull and difficult to decorate interestingly, but if it is covered entirely with mirror it will create an illusory vista.

If mirror is to create a complete illusion, its edges should not show – it should run to the very edge of the wall, up to a door jamb or out of sight behind curtains. If it has to stop where the edges can be seen, they can be disguised

with pilasters, creating an artificial vista or archway. Mirror placed between windows continues the illusion of space, especially since the eye focuses far beyond the wall when looking out of the windows. Behind a sofa or sideboard, an expanse of mirror on the wall will give the impression of space beyond, without disrupting any sense of symmetry or formality created by the arrangement of furniture. Mirror standing alone, covering the wall from floor to ceiling, will create the impression of space opening directly out of the real room which itself then becomes only half of the illusory room. This effect is dramatic and needs to be used with care, but it can be very successful in small hallways and passages.

Above: *Unplastered bricks painted the colour of clotted cream make a contrasting backdrop for a collection of wood-framed pictures and objects made from wood and terracotta. The pictures are hung in an informal, apparently haphazard fashion, filling the spaces between furniture below and staircase above.*

Opposite: *A battered gilt and stucco mirror frame has a textural beauty which would be unattainable by the brand new. Below it is a tureen on a shabby pedestal. A beribboned straw hat and pot of sinewy old geraniums complete the still life set against walls scrubbed with a final ochre wash.*

Framed mirrors create more subtle changes in apparent space, but are often decorative objects that make a distinct contribution to the character of a room. Different styles of frame create different effects. An antique mirror with a carved and gilded frame, peeling and chipped in places, and with the glass mottled by age, gives an impression of romantically crumbling elegance, while an old maple frame with narrow gilt slip is comfortably countrified. A handpainted flat wooden frame has an air of creative bohemianism and a plain pine frame looks clean and utilitarian. An overmantel mirror incorporating shelves at various heights around the mirror is designed to display objects which will themselves frame

Right: *Attention is drawn here to the single picture hung in striking isolation above the settee, while the three hung above one another on the right act as an exclamation mark to the arrangement.*

Right bottom: *Three large and colourful prints by the same artist, identically framed, fill the space between ceiling and sideboard. The arrangement of objects beneath gives an asymmetrical accent.*

the reflected images. A mirror can be used to provide a visual link between objects in the room and wall decoration if its frame picks up motifs or a colour scheme. A black or red lacquer frame, for example, will provide a link with other lacquer objects in an orientally-inspired interior.

Hung where it will reflect light, a mirror can make a dark corner or a dark room seem less oppressive. The ideal position is over a fireplace or over some other piece of furniture where the mirror becomes a centre-piece on the wall and is incorporated into a hanging arrangement of pictures or decorative objects like plates. In fact, for the purpose of hanging, a mirror should be considered to be just another picture. Pairs of mirrors are useful, as are pairs of pictures, but in general mirrors come singly and are fairly large, and for this reason act as a pivot for other hangings.

PICTURES

Picture hanging should be thought about with the whole house in mind. It is a serious business, since its implications for the appearance and character of each room are enormous, but it is also one of the most enjoyable tasks involved in creating a home since it is primarily a matter of organizing beautiful and interesting images to show them off to maximum effect. How you begin depends on what sort of pictures you have and whether they are already framed. If you want to have pictures framed, consider how this can be done to best effect in terms of the picture, and in relation to the decorations in your home. Think also about the possible impact of many images framed in a variety of different ways or identically to look like a collection.

Silvery chrome frames, suitable for a clean modern interior, will not look their best in a richly coloured house furnished with antiques (though they might do in a kitchen or bathroom in such a house). On the other hand,

Left: *Startlingly orange walls throw a formal arrangement of pictures into relief. The paintings are all roughly the same size and are hung according to subject with flowers above and landscapes below, either side of a wall-mounted fretwork egg rack.*

Left bottom: *A vase of country flowers links the furniture below with the single large painting above – an unframed canvas nailed directly on to the white wall.*

plain wooden framing, available in lengths from home improvement stores, painted dark red or green will contribute to the overall decorative scheme in this house without involving enormous expenditure. Cheap or ugly frames can be transformed by a coat of paint in a colour which links them to the rest of the room. Black-and-white images – photographs and engravings for example – look restrained and elegant in slim black frames hung at regular intervals on a wall or in a passage, while strong and brightly coloured images can take a more ornate and elaborate type of frame.

Once all your pictures are framed and assembled, decide on the theme or a type of picture for each room, then consider each room's focal point or points, and allocate a picture to each of these key places. An overmantel or chimney-breast needs a significant picture, as does the wall opposite the entrance to a room. If a mirror is placed in either of these positions, the wall opposite it should be hung with an interesting picture or arrangement of pictures. A large picture should only be hung where the viewer can stand sufficiently far back to be able to see it properly. It will make a narrow space seem wider if it is hung on the wall at one end of it rather than along one side.

Once the focal points have been provided with pictures, you have to decide where the rest of the pictures are to be hung. If you have a great many pictures, this requires careful planning. By all means crowd them together in some rooms, but leave other rooms with fewer pictures and plenty of bare wall around them to create a breathing space, as it were. (Bear in mind subject matter when allocating pictures to specific rooms; pictures of battles or sporting scenes might not be the best choice for a woman's bedroom!) If you have just a few pictures of no great size, the effect will be warmer and bolder if you hang them in a group rather than isolating them individually.

An attractive group will create interest on the wall and will also draw attention to the merits of the individual pieces. The same pictures scattered blandly or jumbled together around the room will hardly be noticed. Collections of pictures of one subject will make the greatest impact gathered together in one room. Paintings, drawings, prints and photographs can be happily mixed together on one wall – this was popular in Victorian homes, even though arbiters of taste pronounced against it. Other considerations like variety and regularity of size and shape and similarity of period and mood are more important than the pictures' medium.

Picture groups can be symmetrical or asymmetrical. Symmetrical arrangements are much easier to get right, but are not always the most effective and depend for success upon having pictures that can be roughly (or exactly) paired by size, shape and content. A typical group on a large wall might have a large painting in the middle, hung so that its centre is just above eye level. Below it, with 2.5–5 cm (1–2 in) of wall between, is a horizontal picture, not so wide as the first and much less deep. On each side of the main picture, a smaller round picture is hung above a square one. Beyond these, to each side, are several much smaller silhouettes, engravings or framed postcards.

The height at which to hang pictures is a matter of common sense – they should not be hung so high up the wall that they cannot be seen. In a room with high ceilings it is tempting to hang pictures according to the proportions of the room, but this will mean that they will be too far from the viewer. Do not be afraid of hanging pictures above one another for effect – this arrangement will allow you to make the most of a few pictures.

The success of an asymmetrical picture grouping depends upon the creation of strong axes. Imagine a large invisible '+' or 'L' drawn on your wall, and hang pictures grouped along these axes, ensuring that no picture edge breaks the lines. This group will, like a symmetrical one, make most impact if there is an obvious focus in the form of a picture larger than the others, accompanied by others of contrasting size. More daring asymmetrical groups can be successfully made with contemporary pictures and prints than with more traditional and antique ones.

When planning the hanging position of pictures that will be seen from another room or an approaching hall or passage, consider the ways in which visual links and differences can be emphasized by similar and contrasting types of picture and frame. Several pictures framed identically will provide a link between rooms if they are hung on the wall by the door in one room and on the part of the wall in the other room that is framed by the door. This method of visual management also applies to single rooms where one part has a different use to another. In a long narrow living room, for example, where one end is used as a dining room and the other as a sitting room, the different functions can be subtly emphasized and the long space gently broken up by hanging black-and-white prints at the dining end and colourful pictures at the sitting end.

When considering any such scheme, it is a good idea not to hang the pictures immediately but to prop them up or lay them flat around the room until you are satisfied with the arrangement. If this does not work for you, make small paper cut-outs imitating your pictures and rearrange them on a large sheet of paper until you are happy with a scheme for hanging them.

There are various methods of hanging pictures. The most common is the brass picture hook from which pictures are suspended by wire or cord looped across their backs. A similar method is to hang a picture from two nails corresponding to a brass ring on each side of the back of the frame. Very heavy pictures may need to be screwed to the wall. If there is a picture rail, pictures can be hung from it on chain, wire or coloured cord (chosen in sympathy with the room's colour scheme). Smaller pictures can be prettily hung from the rail with ribbon.

It is not only pictures, of course, that make attractive wall decoration. Textiles of all sorts, from garments like antique oriental coats, to embroideries, tapestries, kelims and even quilts make original and attractive wall-coverings. They need to be hung with sufficient support to prevent deterioration, however, so you should consult an expert before displaying them. All sorts of objects like plates, china and baskets can be hung on the wall to stunning effect, a subject tackled more fully in the chapter discussing display (pages 89–97).

Left: *Gilt-framed prints, hung formally above each other and close together, act as a visual link between two rooms. Notice the brave placing of a mirror on the floor under the console table.*

DOORS

'Come when you're called;
And do as you're bid;
Shut the door after you;
And you'll never be chid.'

Maria Edgeworth
The Contrast

The door is among man's simplest and cleverest inventions. Basically a means of stopping up a hole in the wall, a door is, of course, much more than just that. It is an entrance to a room when open and a barrier when closed. An open door creates a welcome; it is a visual link between one space and another. Closed, it transforms a house or a room into a single private space at the same time as keeping out draughts and unwanted light, sounds and sights. When seclusion is what you want, the closed (and perhaps locked) door acts as a protective shield, keeping the world at bay.

In visual terms the door into a room is a focus; together with windows, doors provide the walls' punctuation, creating variety and movement. In grand houses over the centuries doors have been given magnificent decoration: at one time they were crowned with dignified heads composed of tiers of carved and gilded architraves surmounted by elaborate pediments. A sense of importance can be achieved on a more modest scale ▶

Opposite: *The beaded architrave surround of this door has been incorporated into a boldly painted scheme – a classical pediment and pillars decorated with strings of circular shapes – which increases the importance of the door itself.*
Right: *A modern double sliding door has been painted in shades of red like a contemporary work of art.*

with a simple architrave, or by hanging a noticeable picture or object above the door. Several doors in one room or hallway can be linked by placing different examples of the same type or shape of picture or object above them. A collector of fans or stuffed birds, for instance, could display an eye-catching fan or a small case of stuffed birds over each door opening off a hallway or room. But any object of suitable size that does not need close examination will look effective in this position.

The starting point for deciding what treatment to give your doors is to establish what they are. If you are lucky, they will be original to the house and therefore of the most appropriate materials, design and proportions. Some original doors may have been boarded over in the manner so popular in post-war years. In this case, it is simply a matter of removing the boards and the paint previously applied to the door (if you like the original colour, you could repaint it in a similar shade). Even if you have only one original door, it can act as a pattern for any replacements.

A building that has been subject at some point to the enthusiasm of a 'modernizer' is quite likely to have a collection of flush doors. Lightweight and hollow, these may appear at

Above: *Glass-paned French windows open on to a courtyard, leading the eye and the imagination beyond the confines of the kitchen. Doors, windows and fire surround are all painted the same restful green.*

Above right: *The upper and lower panels of this door were painted by Duncan Grant for the study at Charleston Farmhouse, where every room has been embellished by Grant, Vanessa Bell and friends.*

Opposite: *Double folding doors offer an elegant solution to problems of space as they fold back neatly on themselves. The two vertical radiators on the opposite wall double as heated towel rails.*

first glance to be unremittingly nasty, but they should not be dismissed out of hand. Replacing them with period panel doors that fit will probably be difficult and expensive. An alternative is to keep the doors and transform them with beading. A reputable timber merchant or home improvement store will offer a range of wooden beading in different widths and shapes which you can buy by the length.

You or your joiner can simply reproduce on your doors the number and shape of panels appropriate to the style and period of the building with mitred beading. If you are adapting all your doors in this way, you could apply your own design. In either case, beware of meanness: beading is easily swallowed up by the overall area of a door, so it is advisable to choose a wider rather than a narrower type. Once the beading is applied, the doors can be painted.

The colour of a door is another important consideration. Often the colour of the skirting (baseboard) is continued up around the door jamb and architrave. The door itself can be painted in the same colour, or in another one that matches or complements the walls. There is a narrow line between decorating a door in keeping with the rest of the room, and causing it to blend in so well that it disappears. Unless this really is your intention, it is worth making doors points of interest. A door's features can be emphasized with paintwork in contrasting colours, or the whole door covered with a decorative finish such as marbling or woodgraining. Where several doors lead off a single space, they should be decorated alike; a simple treatment, which is consistent with other decorations, will prevent the whole space looking fussy or claustrophobic.

One of the simplest ways to treat a door is to oil or polish the bare wood. Although this would not have been done in eighteenth- and nineteenth-century houses, in which the woodwork would have been painted, it can look handsome in a house where much of the furniture is of polished wood. A mixture of raw linseed oil and button polish applied with a cloth feeds bare woodwork and will give a door a rich sheen. If your doors are mahogany, treat them with beeswax and they will respond with an incomparable deep reddish glow. Ordinary bare wood can be stained. This no longer means choosing between stain in various dreary shades of brown; the choice of colours now available makes stain a serious alternative to paint if you want a door to tone in with colours already in a room.

PROBLEM AREAS

Doors can do much more than simply provide a means of entering and leaving a room. They can provide help with the problem of awkward spaces. A long narrow room, for example, can be transformed into two connecting spaces each with more satisfactory proportions by the addition of double or folding doors. These need not be placed directly in the middle of the room, but can be positioned slightly nearer one end or the other, depending on the use of the two parts. Folding doors can be folded away, but need wall-space to fold back against, whereas double doors set into a rigid surround create more of a vista. In a severely limited area a different sort of double door, achieved by dividing the existing door down the middle, is a possible solution as the door does not need so much space into which to open. Another tidy solution where space is limited is to take the doors off their hinges and set them on runners to slide. The most discreet sliding doors disappear into the wall, but this arrangement has to be planned at the construction stage of decorating. The smoothest and quietest sliding doors are those hung from above rather than the ones that grate along the floor in a groove.

FRENCH WINDOWS

Another form of door with interesting possibilities is the French window. A garden or balcony will lend an illusion of greater space to a room (and can be enjoyed all year round) if a solid door, or one with frosted glass, is replaced with French windows. These glass-

paned double doors evoke paintings by Matisse and Dufy of languid Mediterranean afternoons. Tall windows are more elegant than squat ones by virtue of their shape, and French windows have the added attraction of increasing natural daylight.

HATCHES

A much maligned but immensely practical form of opening between one room and another is the hatch. This is usually a

Right: A sunny, Mediterranean or Caribbean feel is created by the brilliant blue of these double doors with louvred panels, set in a plain white wall. The blue is accented by the picture to the left.

Below: A sliding door is suspended from a sturdy iron runner. Bleached wooden cladding on the walls is echoed on the door's lower panel where it provides a visual link and balances the glass panes.

Above: The entrance from a small lobby into the main room has no doors but has been magnificently decorated with an asymmetrical curtain, made from deep glossy silk and swagged theatrically across a pole.

rectangular hole in the wall at table-height between kitchen and dining room for the purpose of passing food and dishes between the rooms. Most hatches have doors for the practical reason that these block out the sights, sounds and smells of the kitchen. The doors can be decorated in several ways. If you want to disguise them, they can be decorated identically to the wall. (The most discreet handles are glass knobs, recessed handles, painted wooden knobs that hardly show, and magnetic touch-sensitive catches, which need to be accompanied by finger-plates.) An alternative method of decoration is to reproduce on a smaller and subtler scale the room's other full-size doors. Hatch doors are

not generally candidates for flamboyant, attention-attracting treatment – they are useful but not at all glamorous. On the other hand, it could be appropriate to make them more interesting by constructing them as screens rather than solid doors, so long as their practical purpose is not forgotten. They could, for instance, be inset with panels of period or reproduction stained or painted glass.

DOOR CURTAINS

No room's decorative scheme should be limited by the necessity for a door. It is perfectly possible to do without one, so long as the practical consequences are recognized and are acceptable. Some of a door's functions can be performed by other devices, such as a decorative folding screen or a curtain.

A door-curtain can be made from two fabrics so that each matches the room on its side of the doorway. An alternative is to have two curtains, one facing each room. One of the attractions of using a curtain to replace a door is its potential for drama. A deeply fringed velvet curtain is demonstrably luxurious as is a swagged and billowing brocade or silk one in a public room like a drawing room, where the expense may be justified. When choosing a treatment for a door-curtain – or curtains – it is worth remembering that it will blend in completely if it is identical to those covering the windows, complete with pelmet (cornice). Nineteenth-century decorators were keen on curtains in doorways, especially those known as *portières* which hung over doors to act as extra draught-proofing. When used on the inside of a door, a *portière* was hung from a hinged brass rod, which swung open with the door.

DOOR FURNITURE

Original doors may not have their original knobs or handles, but there is a huge range of modern and antique door knobs, handles, finger-plates and locks available. The choice of material includes brass, other metals, wood, china and glass. Wooden knobs can be stained or painted, but need to be given many coats of hard varnish, unless gloss paint is used, to make them suitably hard-wearing – otherwise they will discolour with handling. Painted wooden knobs need not be plain – they can be decorated with any pattern or picture, or indeed any cut-out or transfer, that will fit their small surface.

Finger-plates offer an opportunity for decoration with few practical considerations: they simply have to be fixed in the right place on the door (above the handle), and to be made of a material that will protect the door itself. Glass plates are neutral, and at the other extreme it is possible to find curious antique plates embossed with advertisements – a pre-war version of today's logo-emblazoned shopping bag. Locks incorporated into the back-plate of the handle or separate from it

Above: *A tall glass-paned door is shaded by a clever combination of* portière *and ruched blind. The blind-cum-curtain can be raised and lowered and is hung from a hinged brass rod which swings open with the door.*

Opposite: *These double doors are original to the house but similar ones can be constructed to organize a long space into two smaller and more versatile ones. Note also the curved curtain pole fitted over the French windows.*

can adorn a door, as can bolts. Hinges too can be decorative, especially iron ones in early houses where the strap attached to the door is shaped like an arrow or extended heart and stretches right across the door like an embracing arm.

Period and scale are two important considerations when choosing door furniture. Seventeenth-century cottage doors would clearly look unhappy with elegant eighteenth-century brass door knobs – wooden or metal latches would be more appropriate. While door furniture should be in keeping with the style of the doors and building, too rigid an adherence to period can be restricting. Simplicity is a faithful guide, and in a modern house severity is effective.

There are many finishing touches for a home that can be designed and made for you by a craftsman, and door furniture is one of them. Because a door is a practical thing that is much used, original door furniture will contribute to the overall character of a home in an unobtrusive way. It is worth assuring yourself before you begin, however, that your craftsman fully understands the technical requirements of a door knob or handle so that it will actually work. It is also worth considering the logistics of installation. If, for example, your doors are equipped with handles you press down on and you wish to replace them with knobs that you turn, it is likely that the entire workings inside the door will have to be replaced and relocated. There will not be sufficient room for a knob to be turned without your grating your knuckles on the door jamb. Knobs should also be chosen with the weight of the door in mind. A knob on the inside of a heavy front door should be sufficiently strong to bear the extra weight of the door.

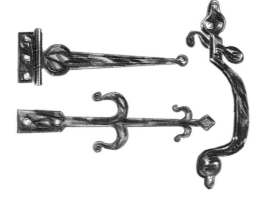

Door furniture is available in a variety of interesting styles to suit all types and periods of home. Materials include brass (left), iron (above) and china (right).

WINDOWS

'Windows are a legitimate field for the exercise of original taste.'

Eliza Haweis
The Art of Decoration 1889

Windows are more varied in appearance than doors. They can be tiny or enormous, square, round, rectangular or any other shape, subdivided crossways or divided by glazing bars into squares or diamonds. In houses that were built with defence in mind, windows are sometimes not much more than peepholes, whereas in modern buildings they sometimes fill the wall. Window shapes are usually a consequence of the period and style in which the house was built, and are in proportion to the size, shape and use of the rooms within.

Opposite: *Simple semi-transparent Roman blinds are visually dynamic because of their bold 'V' shape. The contrast with dark polished antique furniture is successful since other decorations are plain and pale. Notice the wooden column used as a jardinière.*
Right: *A stencilled pattern of roses replaces frosted glass in a first-floor window.*

A seventeenth-century weaver's cottage, for instance, has a long row of narrow top-floor windows originally designed to allow the maximum amount of light in to reach the looms. The main floor of a Georgian country house, by contrast, has windows the generous height of which is greater than the entire floor-to-ceiling measurement in the cottage rooms.

No longer constructed for defensive purposes, windows today simply let the light in and, for the person indoors, frame a view of the outside world. ▶

Their treatment offers enormous scope to the imaginative decorator. A carpet has pieces of furniture placed on it, which distract from its overall form, a ceiling is rarely looked at, unless it has interesting plasterwork, but windows are an immediate focus for the eye. They need to be decorated in a style that complements their form as well as the room's overall decorative scheme.

Before making any decision about how to decorate your windows, it is worth trying to set aside any preconceptions you may have concerning them. Windows need not have curtains, for instance. They may have shutters or blinds or be left uncovered – in a drawing room or dining room where the night-time view

Above: Large and elaborate pelmets need not be stiff and formal. These are softly swagged across a pair of large windows, with long curtains draping on the floor, their fullness billowing out from tie-backs.

is particularly beautiful, for instance, or in a starkly simple interior. Good double glazing will help keep cold air out to compensate for lack of curtains, and as much can be achieved by the clever use of painted colour on and around a window as with acres of expensive fabric. Elaborate pelmets (cornices) and tie-backs need not be heavy and lifelessly correct. With the right approach and success-

ful choice of materials, they can be lively and dramatic and even can be wildly asymmetrical rather than stiffly formal.

If you decide to have curtains, they should generally be of a colour similar to or darker than the surrounding walls, they should extend beyond the sides of the window, to hide them, and they should fall to the floor. Curtains that stop a short distance above the floor are in danger of looking skimpy, and the fabric will hang rigidly rather than softly. Such curtains will also fail in one of their primary functions, which is to exclude every source of draught. However, a very small window will look absurd with long curtains, and on a very tall one long curtains may be difficult to

manoeuvre if they drag too luxuriously on the floor. If your budget does not run to full and appropriately long curtains, it is better to do without them altogether and consider less expensive alternatives.

It may be difficult to decide on an appropriate window treatment. An easy method of clarifying your ideas is to draw a simple picture of the wall, showing its shape and the rough size and position of the windows, to repeat this outline on several separate sheets of paper and then on each one to colour in a different arrangement of blinds, curtains and pelmets. Pin these up in the room and look at them from time to time until you are sure which one you like best and think is most appropriate to the room. Factors to take into consideration include the period of the house, the style of your furniture and the materials from which it is made, the use to which the room is put, its other decorations, and the window itself. When choosing a particular fabric for curtains,

Above left: *Each inside edge of these curtains has been trimmed with a boldly patterned border which is repeated on the pelmet and continued on the walls. The pelmet's lower edge is cut into smart points.*

Above right: *A basement window (or an unsightly view such as a blank wall) can be masked with patterned glass and used for storing glasses which look pretty against the light, stacked on glass shelves.*

remember that it will be virtually back-lit during the day and may appear darker at that time than when artificial light is shining directly on to it in the evening.

A window's structure consists of the glass, the frame and the surround. In a room where the view is less than desirable, this can be masked by decorating the window glass. You can have a pane of etched glass made by a

craftsman and can either replace the clear glass with it, or simply hang it over the existing glass (in which case you can move the pane when you want and take it with you if you move house). Alternatives are glass panels decorated with painting or constructed from coloured glass, showing either figurative subjects, geometric patterns or a mixture of the two. In Victorian houses the borders of windows and glass doors (and sometimes a larger area) frequently incorporate etched, coloured and painted glass squares or rectangles decorated with geometric patterns or scenes of birds and animals. An antique glass panel of this type can be bought and then propped on the sill of a small window or hung over the existing glass – it will be seen much better back-lit in this way than if hung in a frame on the wall like a picture.

Window fastenings are frequently dictated by security requirements, but sometimes locks can be separate from catches so that some choice is possible in the latter. Utilitarian window catches that are plain black are often smart, brass catches are handsome on eighteenth- and nineteenth-century windows and painted iron on earlier windows and cottage windows. The most charming casement-window catch is that made of iron which ends not in a stump but with a twirl or a neat coil. Sash windows may rattle if not secured with a tightly fastening catch. Fastenings on modern windows are among the ugliest and most beautiful, depending on the designer.

Window frames are generally made of wood or metal, although plastic frames that never need to be painted are installed in many new houses and often used for replacement windows. Wood frames need to be protected with paint or varnish, especially on the outside. Indoors, they can be painted or stained any colour. This need not be brilliant white – pale shades of colours like yellow and grey give a similar effect but are more interesting – almost any shade, dark or light, of any colour can be used to continue the room's overall decorations. The colour can be chosen to provide a link with the curtain fabric, and it can be continued around the rest of the room's woodwork such as on the skirting (baseboard) and doors. Bare wooden windows can be varnished, oiled or stained, but the woodwork needs to be in good condition.

SHUTTERS

Indoor shutters have been part of windows for as long as windows have existed, and certainly much longer than glass (which to some extent replaced them). Shutters slid into or folded back against the wall or were drawn up like sashes when not in use. They served to keep out the cold air and, even with glass in the windows, fulfil the same useful function today with the added attraction of deterring burglars and other intruders. More sophisticated folding types have upper and lower sections that can be closed independently of each other, so that light and air can be let in above while privacy is maintained by the lower part being closed.

Shutters have not always been considered fashionable, but when out of favour they have not necessarily been removed by previous owners of a house but simply nailed into the window splay on each side and painted over. It is well worth restoring such shutters to use. With a little work it should be easy to release them and a joiner can be commissioned to do any repairs. Shutters can be oiled, varnished

Decorative fastenings can be fitted to casement, sash and French windows.

or painted, depending on the rest of the window decoration. In addition to their practical advantages, shutters are incomparably handsome. If they do their draught-excluding job properly there is no need for curtains, except for the sake of appearance which may well be better served, however, by leaving the shutters exposed if they are handsome.

CURTAINS AND BLINDS

Privacy is one of the primary requirements of a comfortable home, particularly in towns and cities. Curtains shut out the outside world after dark, and in the daytime privacy at overlooked windows can be achieved by installing gauze, net or lace curtains. Many people dislike the appearance of net curtains, and they are not suited to some types of interior such as a sixteenth-century cottage or a modernist interior. An alternative is to mount a piece of muslin or opaque gauze flat on to a hinged or removable frame that fits the lower part of a window.

(In a basement apartment it would fit the upper part or the whole of a window.)

Lightly gathered muslin, spotted net or coloured voile can be hung at bedroom windows, or panels of lace hung flat across them. Many fabric designs have accompanying lace that echoes the same pattern, and it is also possible to find ready-made, window-sized, cotton-lace panels. For most types of window, restraint is, as usual, a reliable guide. Patterns, flounces, gathers and extravagant arrangements should be avoided, except perhaps with large windows in a Victorian or Edwardian house, or in a scheme designed intentionally to look cheerfully vulgar.

Curtain fabric should be chosen as part of an overall decorating plan for a room. It is the fabric that will make the greatest impact in the room, being the most visible and it is therefore important to make the right choice. Conversely, if the curtains are inherited or brought from a previous home and are likely to be per-

Above left: An elaborate arrangement of layers of curtain manages to look fresh not fusty. Both the curtains behind and the lace-edged net draped in front are fixed in place, the curtains being tied back with heavy tasselled cords during the day.

Above right: Another clever layered arrangement consists of a plain blind behind an ethereal muslin curtain (both edged with white pom-pom braid), topped with a lace-edged valance.

Opposite: The garden view through this window would be marred by curtains, and in any case the shutters, folded across the window at night, amply fulfil the functions of draught-proofing and privacy.

manent, they should be taken as a starting point for the rest of the room's decorations, or at the very least be taken into serious account.

The choice of the fabric and the style for your curtains should be made slowly. One important consideration is to avoid the extremes of fashion as far as possible. It is extremely difficult to define exactly where fashion stops and taste starts since we are inevitably influenced by current trends, but a visit to a library that has back-numbers of interior-decorating magazines will offer a lesson in what not to do. Look at the issues published ten or 15 years ago – the contemporary fabrics and curtain styles that have dated in the intervening time will leap out at you, compared to those that have not.

The pattern of fabric for curtains should generally relate to the proportions of the room. There are always exceptions, of course, created by people who are gifted decorators or use fabric in a highly imaginative way. Very

small and very large patterns can be difficult to use successfully. Small patterns disappear except in a small room, and in a large room their constituent colours appear to blend together, so that a delicate red print on cream will look pink from a distance. Large patterns can be overwhelming, but can look stunning in a large room or on a tall window. A fabric with a large pattern in an uncomplicated combination of colours, like sky blue on white, will look fresh and cool rather than frightening, whereas a smaller, busier pattern combining dark and hot colours, like navy blue and scarlet, will look more imposing. Scale should not therefore be considered in isolation from colour and design.

Pattern is one of the glories of curtain fabric and no one need be afraid of it. To take refuge in plain unpatterned fabric is entirely in keeping with more ascetic styles of interior decoration, but pattern is invaluable in creating

Above: *Boldly printed black-and-white fabric is put to simple but dramatic use by being draped over the curtain pole in two swags above fixed curtains. The curtains are tied back during the day.*

Opposite: *In this stunning arrangement of a single curtain, tied in the middle with a huge bow, every detail, from the gathers and ribbons at the top to the fullness of the fabric on the floor, has been finely planned.*

cosier and more sophisticated moods. Strong colour can have the same effect. The choice is huge and includes designs created a century or more ago like those rediscovered during the restoration of country houses or, like William Morris fabrics, perennially popular.

Fabric need not be bought new for curtains – auction houses sell second-hand curtains, which may with luck be made from antique fabric or magnificent velvet or silk far beyond most budgets if bought new, and it is also worth looking at the 'small ad' columns in local newspapers. Rugs and carpets can also be used successfully as window and bed curtains, hung from a plain pole or rod.

Practical considerations will affect the amount of fabric needed for curtains and the type of lining required. Curtains are designed to keep warmth in and cold out. In summer they also keep bedrooms dark to allow the occupants to sleep undisturbed after daybreak. None of these functions will be satisfactorily achieved if the curtains are thin and skimpy. In a room that is used for any length of time curtains should ideally be lined and interlined, hung from well above the top of the window (half-way between the window and the ceiling in a regularly proportioned room is the general rule), extend to each side of the window frame and reach the floor or hang well below the window sill.

The ideal fullness for curtains is a subject of some debate and depends on the final effect that you want. A general guide to the amount of fabric needed to make an averagely generous curtain is double the width of the curtain pole or track. More fabric is required for certain types of formal gathering effects such as box and cartridge pleats. It is important to bear in mind what the curtains will look like when closed: too little fabric will result in flattened curtains which look mean; too much fabric will make the curtains difficult to draw back and they take up extra space each side of the window if they are not to block out light.

It is better to make a virtue of necessity if you can only afford a limited amount of fabric. Hang it completely flat in two halves, securing it flat across the top, rather than making a few mean and pathetic-looking gathers. To draw the curtains back, run diagonal drawstrings (attached to the back or sewn into the lining of the curtains) from a point two-thirds of the way down the touching edges to the top outer corners, with tails down the sides for pulling on.

A preconception that can be dismissed is that every window needs two curtains. One curtain can be used very effectively on certain types of window. A window in the corner of a room, for example, might not allow sufficient space to draw a curtain back on each side. A single full curtain looped back asymmetrically with a tie-back during the day will look far more effective than two thin curtains squeezed into the limited space. Asymmetrical arrangements can be applied to any window – a large, long net or lace curtain can be looped back in one direction and the heavier outer curtain swagged across it in the other direction, restrained by a matching tie-back. Alternatively, curtains of the same lightweight fabric can be draped from opposite ends of the window, so that they cross over each other. With such an arrangement the curtains cannot be drawn but, if they are made from a fine fabric like muslin, they can be used to block out an unattractive view without cutting out all the light.

Curtains need not draw back at all – the inverted 'V' shape between fixed curtains draped back during the day can be used to soften a large square window or break up a long dull passage. The curtains use slightly less fabric, are permanently fixed to a batten flush against the wall, and are draped over tie-backs at the sides. In the evenings they can

Opposite: *A single flat curtain with a simple, bold repeat pattern, fixed flat across the top of the window and drawn to one side with a diagonal drawstring, completes the fresh clean look of a bathroom.*

Right: *Pale, diaphanous fabric has been gracefully sculpted into permanently open curtains and pelmets which look light enough to float. The blind hidden behind the pelmet can be lowered when required.*

Below: *By day, a fringed festoon blind is raised to reveal the handsome proportions of a tall window. By night, the lowered blind and closed wooden shutters provide privacy and draught-proofing.*

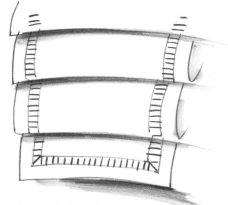

Roller blinds can be decorated with borders and edges, Roman blinds with edging (top left) or paint (centre), to draw them into a decorative scheme.

Left: *Blinds are practical and versatile. Different types and colours can be used in adjacent spaces. Hung over outside doors, blinds will act like* portières *when lowered, helping to exclude draughts.*

Opposite: *Unlined, washable cotton curtains are practical in a kitchen. Here, a fresh geometric print and simple method of hanging, from a slim rail run through looped tabs, contribute to a countrified look.*

Below: *Long Roman blinds fill tall windows whose height is emphasized by a sheer column of mirror attached to the wall between. Blinds are ideal in an interior which strives after a clean, uncluttered look.*

either be released from the tie-backs and allowed to fall, or a blind in the window recess can be drawn down. This combination is particularly effective if the blind contrasts with the curtain fabric – the former striped or plaid, the latter plain or floral for example – and if the bottom of the blind is given an interesting shape. Castellations, scallops, deep loops, long points or triangles are alternative shapes for the bottom line, which can be finished off with braid or tassels. If you give the blind a shaped edge, make it bold rather than small and insignificant.

The combination of curtains and blinds can also be used to make the most of a limited amount of expensive fabric. If you swag the fabric across the top of the window and drape it down the sides, the practical task of shutting out light and cold can be achieved by heavy blinds, perhaps with the additional help of muslin or net curtains between the blind and the room. The different layers revealed in this way will make the windows more interesting.

Blinds are almost as varied in style as curtains and do not need to be made from fabric. Ones which are, however, vary from severely folded Roman blinds to the fuller, gathered festoon or Austrian blinds. The latter were popular in wealthy Georgian houses because they could be raised out of reach of candle flames where curtains might have been a fire hazard. The same applies today in a dining room frequently lit by candles. Fabric blinds can be made from your own material to match or contrast with curtains and other decorations, or they can be bought in a wide range of plain colours, from cream and white through pastel shades to brilliant and rich tones which make a positive contribution to an interior. It is also possible to buy or commission blinds decorated with a picture – these were popular in the nineteenth century when they were often painted or printed on opaque material, which gave the picture added luminosity as light shone through it from outside.

Blinds are more versatile than they are often given credit for, and one type or another will suit almost any interior. They are a particular asset if you want a streamlined look and in steamy functional rooms such as kitchens and bathrooms where curtains would be considered by some to be unhygienic. Semitransparent blinds are also useful for protecting fine furniture and pictures from direct sunlight during the day. (Blinds can also be used to hide the contents of shelves, or to divide one part of a room from another.) Nonfabric blinds include Venetian blinds made of wood or metal, and bamboo and split-cane blinds. None of these will completely exclude the light – except perhaps a closed Venetian blind – so they can all be used to mask an unwelcome view. No blinds are draughtproof, particularly slatted ones, and they are obviously not as successful as curtains at keeping a room warm.

CURTAIN POLES

A major decision when choosing curtains is the choice of fixture from which they will hang. Poles and rods with rings are attractive but unpopular with some people who find the curtains less easy to draw, especially if the window is tall, than if they are on a track. There are poles available, however, which have a runner and drawing mechanism concealed inside and operated with strings which hang down from one end. Curtain poles have great decorative potential. They can be covered in fabric or have fabric swagged and draped over them in symmetrical or asymmetrical arrangements, and thus supply a foundation for a range of dramatic curtain heads.

Slim brass rods, attached to the wall at each end, are sufficient to take the weight of curtains at a small window, but a larger heavy pole of any length will need supportive brackets at intervals and so will stand proud of the window. Curtains hung from such poles have the disadvantage of not completely sealing

the window from draughts. This is less important in a hall or landing than it is in a sitting room, for instance, where you may find that guests who start a winter evening sitting by the window have migrated to the other side of the room before the evening is over.

PELMETS

One answer to draughts is to have a pelmet (cornice), with the curtains hung from a metal or plastic track concealed behind it. Pelmets have the added attraction of making windows look formal and finished and open up a mass of decorative possibilities. They can be made from almost any material including the same fabric as the curtains or a contrasting fabric, deep fringing, carved and painted wood,

paper-covered wood or board, or any combination of these. The simplest type is the box pelmet – a long, straight, rectangular shape placed across the top of the curtains to cover the track. The most elaborate pelmets imitate Victorian creations and include opulent swags of heavy fabric trimmed with tassels, bobbles or fringes and perhaps crowned with a wooden panel cut into fleur-de-lis or Gothic points. Only a tall window in a grand room could carry such magnificence, but elements can be drawn from pelmets such as these to give an air of grandeur to less spectacular windows in more modest rooms.

Between these two extremes lies the shaped pelmet. This is flat like the box pelmet but its lower edge is shaped into curved

forms, castellations or points, not unlike the bottom edge of a decorative blind. If the curtains have a light, fairly small pattern, the pelmet could be made from the same material with the addition of a wide border along the bottom in the form of twining leaves or swags of flowers, with the pelmet following the swooping lines of the swags. Curtains made from a striped or geometrically patterned fabric could be topped with a pelmet shaped into square castellations, ogee points or inverted Gothic arches. A brocade pelmet might have curved castellated points with a small tassel hanging from each point. Visits to stately homes and other houses open to the public will give you ideas for pelmets, as will books about houses and interior design. The

Opposite: *Finished with tassels, this clever pelmet follows the arched shape of a gothic window. The pelmet and curtain track continue each side of the window so that the curtains do not block daylight.*

Right: *The cool restraint of this bedroom is continued in the curtain fabrics. A narrow but highly decorative pelmet is softened by a full valance. The main curtains drape luxuriously on the floor and privacy is maintained by a plain net half-curtain.*

Below: *A flat antique pelmet hangs far down the sides of the bathroom window. Sheer net provides daytime privacy and a full festoon blind can be lowered at night.*

good-quality interior-decorating magazines also contain a lot of helpful information.

The impression that a pelmet gives of finishing off a window can be achieved in other ways. A wide fabric border can be added to the top of the curtains in a darker colour or possibly a pattern. Curtains hung from a pole with rings can be cuffed – a second layer of the curtain (or other) fabric is attached to the top of the curtains giving the effect of a turn-back like a formal shirt cuff. This layer can be either narrow or deep, in proportion to the height of the curtains.

The valance is another useful decorative device. It is a gathered length of fabric like a very short curtain, hung from a track or pole in front of or behind the curtains. If put behind, it can be made of light, floaty fabric and used in addition to a pelmet for a luxurious effect. In front of curtains, a valance will look like a pelmet, and can in fact be converted to one if it is attached to a pelmet board in the form of a shelf above the window. A valance (and curtain cuffs) need not be straight – it can be shaped in one single curve or in scallops, castellations or points. The depth should always be in generous proportion to the height of the window or it will look silly.

Although pelmets serve a useful purpose in keeping out draughts that creep over the top of curtains, they can be used by themselves, without curtains. A window that does not need to be made private or draught-proof can be decorated with a plain or shaped pel-

met applied directly to the wall and extending just beyond the window recess. Alternatively, it can be fitted into the recess. In either case, the wall surrounding the window can be decorated with painted geometric shapes, stencils or some other simple border, in colours that link the window to the rest of the room.

UNUSUAL WINDOWS

Windows should not necessarily be thought of as single entities. A pair or a row of windows in the same wall will be unified by a long pelmet or pole stretching across their full length. If there are two windows, each can be treated asymmetrically: either each one with a single curtain drawn to opposite sides; or with two curtains drawn into the middle, with lace or net curtains balancing them on the outer edges.

The appearance of a room can be altered with cleverly planned curtains. A long low narrow room with several windows down one side will look long and narrow if each window is treated separately, especially if the curtains are short. The best way to unify the window wall is to reduce the number of curtains (taking the windows in pairs, for example, and giving each window one big curtain only), and to increase their length. Low windows can be disguised by hanging the curtains from well above the top of the window to the floor and by facing the wallspace between window and curtain rail with mirror.

A small, narrow or badly placed window can also be helped with mirror. If it is small or narrow, the sides of the window recess can be faced with mirror cut to fit to generate more light. The ceiling of the window recess can also be lined with mirror, especially if the window is placed high up on the wall.

TIE-BACKS

Whatever the arrangement of curtains, tie-backs are invaluable. In their simplest form these consist of a cord that loops round the curtain and is attached to a hook on the wall. The cord can be decorated with tassels or have other ornaments hanging from it. Fabric tie-backs are usually made in the same fabric as the curtains, in an elongated kidney shape with a brass ring or ribbon-tie at each end to attach it to the hook. Elaborate tie-backs made from plaited fabric ropes are another alternative. The name 'tie-back' also applies to solid restraints such as curved brass brackets, short wooden posts with turned ends and gilded curled acanthus leaves – some types of the handsome and decorative antique tie-backs which are available.

As well as being decorative, tie-backs help make the most of curtains by taking the weight off the fabric so that it can billow and fall in folds. The ideal position in which to place them is somewhere between shoulder and waist height, depending on the length and size of the window.

Left: Identical pelmets swagged across the tops of a pair of windows and falling in folds down the sides frame the garden view beyond. The fabric has been lined to match the green-painted woodwork.

Opposite: Tie-backs are invaluable and handsome. Full, heavy curtains are here drawn back tightly by coloured cord finished with tassels and looped over brass rosettes to reveal an elegant radiator box and grille.

Below: Plain glass in tall French windows is quickly and cleverly enlivened by patterned adhesive strips around the edges of and in crosses across the panes.

CEILINGS

'We cannot afford to ignore the ceiling from the aesthetic point of view. Unadorned or badly treated it becomes painfully obtrusive.'

Guy Cadogan Rothery
Ceiling and their Decorations c.1911

Left: *Fat gold stars on a soft blue ground make this a fairytale ceiling. Emphasizing the contours of the ceiling in this way gives a lift to the whole room, drawing one's eye upwards to the 'heavens'.*
Right: *Beams crisscrossing the ceiling of an old house have been given new life by the application of a bold stencil pattern painted blue-on-white.*

Ceilings have become the poor relations of interior design. Since they are not as visually dominant as walls and are not used as floors are, they have tended to be painted white or cream and forgotten about. When one has little time and a limited budget to spend on decorating, this seems only sensible. After all, it is only in the bedroom and bathroom that you ever really look at the ceiling. But in previous ages ceilings have been viewed as offering unrivalled opportunity for decorations that will be seen as a whole, without rugs, furniture or pictures getting in the way.

The ceiling of the Sistine Chapel in Rome, painted by Michelangelo, is a sublime example of this, as are Robert Adam's eighteenth-century plaster ceilings. These are grand schemes, however, while most of us have to devise a plan for more modest spaces.

Though it may seem less significant, a ceiling is as much part of a room as the walls or floor and makes a quiet contribution to its overall character. There is no reason why the ceiling should be deprived of colour. A light ▶

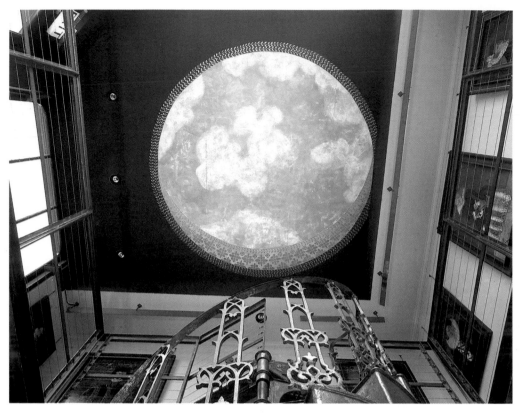

colour complementary to the walls, or perhaps the same colour if the ceiling is broken up by beams or plasterwork, will give it life and warmth. If the ceiling is high and gives the room the appearance of being chilly, you can 'lower' it somewhat by painting it a colour and lower it further still by continuing the colour down the walls as far as a picture rail or border. If the ceiling is low, paint it a pale colour (not necessarily white) and give it a wide painted or paper border. This border will fool the eye into thinking the ceiling is smaller and therefore higher than it is – the same effect that a ceiling cornice produces.

A ceiling with a plasterwork cornice (crown molding) and perhaps a central rose (medallion) has a character of its own that needs to be drawn out. The plaster may be clogged with layers of old paint, like wall cornices (page 10), and need restoration to reveal its three-dimensional qualities. Some ceiling cornices are simple horizontal mouldings, some incorporate classical shapes and motifs or pretty intertwined leaves or flowers. The leaves and flowers can be painted in appropriate colours (an effect the Victorians, who hardly built a house without ceiling decoration, were fond of).

Ceiling plasterwork will be thrown into relief

by a coloured background, and the plasterwork itself can be subtly painted in shades of a subdued colour to show off its detail. Slightly darker shades should be applied to background and deeper detailing, and lighter ones to the most prominent parts. If this is really well done, it will hardly show that it has been painted in different colours, but nonetheless the character and lively detail of the plasterwork will spring magically to life.

Some modern houses and apartments feel like nothing more than a sequence of boxes. One way of making a room more homely, by reducing the number of sharp corners, is to add a simple clean curved coving to the join between walls and ceiling. You should consider carefully before doing this, however, as you are interfering with the architect's intentions by adding architectural detail. If the architect intended the place to be severely modern, it will not be appropriate to add coving, but if it was budget-built utility housing where cost was the primary consideration it may be legitimate to 'interfere' in this way. Keep it simple, though – elaborate mock-Adam classicism will look absurd.

Old houses whose ceilings are crisscrossed with beams pose different problems. Bare timber beams are attractive, but dust

Above left: *The cornice linking ceiling to walls has been painted in strong colours, drawing attention to the height of the walls and leading the eye onwards to the fine plaster mouldings on the ceiling itself.*

Above: *A cast-iron staircase has a hard-wearing, outdoor look so the witty* trompe l'œil *on the ceiling of this stairwell, suggesting the roof is open to a cloudy blue sky, is entirely appropriate.*

Opposite: *Wooden cladding, painted the same cream colour as the walls, brings the ceiling nearer without it becoming overbearing in this restrained room.*

and dirt drop from them. A coat of varnish can help solve this problem but it changes the appearance of the wood. The best solution perhaps is to scrub the wood with warm water and vinegar, which cleans the surface and brings out the grain. The area of ceiling between the beams can be painted a flat colour, or covered with painted decoration. Seventeenth-century ceilings painted in this way show designs varying from bold and simple human figures to intricate leaves and flowers.

This type of decoration can be painted or stencilled on using ordinary emulsion (latex) wall paint in colours that match or complement those in the room's other decorations. Practical difficulties of painting above your head include dripping paint and a stiff neck, but the effort can bring dramatic results.

Any ceiling can be decorated with images. Gold stars or puffy white clouds and wheeling birds painted on a blue ground in imitation of sky transform a ceiling into a piece of delightful whimsy. If you are artistically inclined, you could decorate your ceiling for yourself. Alternatively, if you have a larger budget, you could commission an artist – perhaps a specialist in *trompe l'œil* – to paint a ceiling for you. Subjects historically considered suitable for overhead decoration have included Christian and mythological subjects such as the Ascension of the Virgin and the Fall of Icarus, but a modern ceiling could provide the backdrop for a more modern subject.

Another elaborate treatment is to cover the ceiling with fabric drawn to the centre or draped along the length of the room like a tent. Such a ceiling is generally the prerogative of the wealthy and exotically-minded with a large decorating budget, but can be reproduced with imaginative use of inexpensive materials and a little do-it-yourself ability. Good-quality interior-decorating magazines will give you interesting ideas. Do not forget the implications in case of fire, however.

FLOORS

'We want the floor to be comfortable, warm to the touch, inviting. But we also want it to be hard enough to resist wear, and easy to clean.'

A Pattern Language 1977

Floors get more wear and tear than any other surface in a room. Practicality is therefore always a significant consideration in the choice of one type of floor covering or treatment over another. This does not mean the choice is narrow – on the contrary, the range of finishes and designs is so great that it is necessary to look carefully at the different alternatives and think seriously about what is best. The classic solution is bare polished boards and rugs. Painted floors are hard-wearing and individual. Fitted carpet is easy-care but not cheap. A varied range of natural-fibre matting is now available. 'Old-fashioned' linoleum is actually a wonderfully modern, good-looking material; and punched rubber flooring, is popular in some modern homes. Your choice of floor finish needs to tie in with the period and style of your other decorations, furniture and pictures as well as the life you lead and the extent of your budget.

Floors tend to be constructed from wood or concrete or, in some old houses, from stone. The bare ▶

Left: *Wooden floors throughout this house have been treated differently to define areas with different uses. The far passage has a plain polished floor, whereas in the kitchen tough green paint is decorated with blue stars and geometric shapes.* Right: *Another coloured wooden floor brightens a living room in the same house with a lively regular pattern.*

material in all these cases has several disadvantages. Stone can be damp and dirty and it is cold. Concrete is drab, cold and hard without the natural charms of stone, though it is tough and practical and is transformed when painted with colourful industrial floor paints. Wooden floors are noisy and, unless in good condition, they tend to be unsealed so not only are they draughty, but dirt and dust fall between the boards and under the skirting (baseboard) and tiny objects, such as contact lenses, can easily be lost down the cracks. There are also tile and brick floors, which often have a warm colour and, in the case of brick, a warmer feel than stone. The range of local and imported tiles now available is huge and wonderfully varied, the most traditional being terracotta-coloured quarry tiles. Bricks too come in a variety of colours and finishes. Tile and brick floors can be laid anew in various patterns, but this is perhaps more of a construction job than a finishing touch.

Above: *This remarkable floor has been richly painted and stencilled to look like an intricate Kerman shrub carpet incorporating plants and animals. Finished with heavy varnish, it will withstand considerable wear and tear and can be washed. The disadvantage is you cannot take it with you.*

Opposite: *Large, sweeping geometric shapes on a modern carpet provide the main feature of this sparsely decorated and furnished room.*

A great deal can be done with a wooden floor that appears at first glance to be irredeemably dirty and scruffy, so long as the structure is basically sound. Loose and creaky boards can be screwed down; small gaps can be filled; a few badly damaged boards can be replaced and sanding will remove an astonishing amount of ancient and apparently embedded grime. Whether you are going to stain, wax, oil, varnish, lime or paint the boards, sanding is the vital first step. Sanding can be done either by a professional or you can do it yourself with the aid of a hired sanding machine. It is not a pleasant job, but it is worth doing well as it will enable you to achieve a good finish. Once the floor is sanded and clean, decoration can begin. An alternative, if the boards are irreperably shoddy and perhaps even unsafe, is to cover or replace them with sterling board – heavy-quality chipboard (particleboard) made from crushed pine pieces. This is a strong and hard

material and, once it is sealed with varnish, looks handsome in a modern interior.

How you decorate the floor depends initially on whether it is going to be a strong decorative element in itself, or whether it is going to have rugs and mats laid upon it. If the latter is the case, one overall finish such as wax, stain and varnish or coloured paint is best. The better the boards, the simpler the treatment should be, so that the natural qualities of the wood can be appreciated. Wax is the classic finish, but the wood has to be repolished regularly. Danish oil has a warm colour, is quickly absorbed and is fairly hard-wearing.

Paint is an excellent covering for boards not in perfect condition that have had to be filled and renovated. Choose a colour with character that complements the room's other decorations, but is not so pale or dark that it will show up the dust and fluff which naturally accumulates when a room is used. Bear in mind too the colours in the rugs you are going

to lay over the painted floor and avoid a colour that will overwhelm them. A colour taken from one of them will probably be ideal.

If the floor is to be uncovered, a world of pattern and colour opens up. Big, bold painted geometric shapes can be contained by a border around the edge of the floor; subtle lines and checks are elegant and sophisticated, as is a marble-effect finish. Other paint techniques that are effective include stencilling or a *trompe l'œil* imitation of the rich colours and patterns of an oriental carpet. Painting a pattern on a floor involves a good deal of work but the result is often stunning. Patterns involving different coloured stains should be kept fairly simple as stain has been known to blur and run, drawn through the grain by natural absorption.

FLOOR COVERINGS
A rug laid on bare boards should be protected by a piece of good underlay cut slightly

smaller than its own size. Rugs can of course be laid on other flooring besides bare boards. Plain carpet provides the warmest possible background, whereas rush or other natural-fibre matting gives a slightly rougher look and is especially appropriate in modern houses or very old houses, which would originally have had loose rushes strewn on the earth floor to restrict the rising dust. The choice of type and finish of natural-fibre matting varies hugely from a very loose and coarse weave to a soft and fine carpeting suited to the most sophisticated interior. Colours vary too: as well as the range of natural buffs and browns, some matting is now dyed to colours including a stunning rich red. Some types of matting are extremely hard-wearing but all matting tends to be slippery so would be unsuitable for stairs. Kitchens and bathrooms are not ideal rooms for natural-fibre matting since it dries slowly when wet, and neither are children's bedrooms as it feels prickly to their feet.

One great advantage that rugs have over fitted carpet (in general) is that you can take them with you when you move, and change them when you feel like it in the meantime. The varied colours and patterns of rugs contribute more positively to an interior than plain carpet, which does not draw attention to itself. In a modern house with white walls, a bold modern rug incorporating vivid colours and dynamic shapes can be the main source of decorative interest. A home filled with antique wooden furniture is an appropriate setting for Persian or Turkey rugs. Geometrically patterned and vibrantly coloured, the flat-woven kelim has a contribution to make in almost every type of interior. Colours vary from pale and delicate pinks and blues to deep and robust reds, blues and greys. Such is their popularity that lengths of kelim are now used to upholster furniture like sofas, chairs and stools, and smaller pieces are made into cushions. The resulting effect is rich and exotic – a far cry from frills and flowered chintz.

Wall-to-wall carpeting began to be more widely available in the nineteenth century as a result of the Industrial Revolution and is, today, one of the most luxurious ways of covering floors. Carpet is plain or patterned.

Above: Linoleum shakes off its fuddy-duddy image to imitate classic marble tile flooring – but it is softer and warmer to the touch while being practical and durable.

Opposite: An exceptionally luxurious wooden floor, inlaid in framed squares before being polished to a rich sheen, is bare of rugs or carpet. A similar result could be achieved on ordinary boards with paint or careful application of stain.

The traditional view of patterned carpet is of something horribly vulgar covered in lurid swirling flowers, but not all patterned carpets are like this. Many incorporate elegantly restrained geometric designs, traditional motifs like the fleur-de-lis or heraldic symbols in colours that are simple and clean. Good-quality patterned carpet of this type is sophisticated and tends to be much more expensive than a plain, coloured carpet. Plain carpets in an uninspiring colour can be drearily dull. If you move to a new house already fitted with serviceable but dreary plain carpet, try covering it up with rugs in the main rooms before going to the drastic measure of removing it. It will

keep you warm and you may find you can live with it. Beware of over-compensating in your choice of colour on the walls for fear you end up emphasizing the drabness of the carpet.

An alternative to the rug, in rooms like kitchens, bathrooms and playrooms where there is likely to be a certain amount of splashing and spilling, is the oilcloth. Before carpet was widely available, oilcloths were frequently used to decorate and protect wooden and stone floors and were sometimes painted in imitation of those materials. Made from canvas covered in layers of paint thickened with linseed oil, oilcloths were fairly hard-wearing and waterproof and were the forerunners of linoleum which was introduced in 1860. Linoleum is a tough and hard-wearing material with hessian (burlap) backing, and is ideal for kitchens and bathrooms. (In a bathroom the bath box can be covered with it and so can the walls, so long as the edges are thoroughly sealed.) Made in a variety of qualities and a huge range of colours, linoleum can be laid in cheerful chequerboard patterns or with elaborate inset borders. Modern vinyls are softer than linoleum and not as tough, but are made in imitation of a wide range of other materials like tiling and wooden parquet.

FIREPLACES AND RADIATORS

'...sunlight and a hot blazing fire are the best kinds of heat.'

A Pattern Language 1977

One of the criteria of a comfortable home is that it should be warm. Unfortunately, the contraptions which make up a modern central heating system though efficient are not beautiful. The opposite is true of a fireplace with a lit fire in it. But, while it is a welcome sight and one that gives a room a focus, the open fire is a notably inefficient form of heating. One way to achieve effective heating and an inviting atmosphere is to combine open fires with central heating to provide warmth throughout the house or apartment.

Left: *A plain slate or wooden fireplace can be decorated with a figurative scene of local life, including you and your family. Objects on the mantelshelf are here arranged symmetrically, and logs and fire irons are neatly stored within the fender.* Right: *A single fine object on a marble mantelpiece complements rich but restrained colours and patterns.*

A fireplace can be replaced if you cannot live with it, although if original it will reflect the period of the house. Where a fireplace has been removed and the hole boarded over, a new one can be installed providing the chimney is not closed. Such alterations necessarily involve disruption and obviously need to be completed well before the decorating stage. If you retain an old fireplace, however, you may want to remove later decoration from it to restore it to its original condition. Taste can change dramatically and it is ▶

hard to imagine now that in the 1920s, the British magazine *Homes & Gardens* proposed that 'displeasing' Victorian tiles set into a cast-iron fire-surround should be painted black.

Often it is simply not possible, or not desirable, to return things to exactly the way they were. Over centuries, or even decades, different owners make structural alterations and one of their first targets is often the fireplace. The result can be an upset system. Chimneys and fireplaces are notoriously tricky: there are technical requirements for a working fire, such as a correct relationship between the area open to the room and the size of the flue or chimney. If, for instance, you have a massive open grate which would accommodate a range, but a modern, narrow-diameter chimney liner has been fitted, there could be a serious problem and a specialist should be consulted before you make a decision about what to install.

The chimney-piece and size of the fireplace opening are structural and difficult to alter, but there is scope in the type of grate that can be fitted. The obvious first choice is a grate of the appropriate period for the fireplace and the building. A large open grate can be looked upon as an asset rather than a problem, as long as the fire draws properly. Logs can be stored nearby to dry thoroughly, either stacked up by the side or in a log basket (placed where it is not a fire hazard). Flowers and herbs can be dried in the fireplace, hanging from a frame if there is sufficient space. Coal can be stored in a scuttle of iron or brass or decorative papier mâché. Fire irons such as tongs and a poker are necessary for maintaining a fire and should be chosen to suit the scale and type of the fire-surround. Mostly these are made in sets with a shovel and perhaps a brush for sweeping up stray ashes. A trivet or stand on which to put a kettle or tea pot, near the fire where it can keep warm, is a useful piece of fireplace furniture for a drawing or sitting room.

Before the advent of central heating and electric light, the firescreen was a vital accessory for protecting the complexion against the heat of the fire. After dark the fire was also an important source of light, but it was necessary to sit close to it to benefit from the glow. A firescreen was either held in the hand like a stiff flat fan, or it took the form of a freestanding panel or a panel attached to a pole so that it could be adjusted to the right height, leaving both hands free for sewing or playing cards. Though they are no longer so necessary in

Above: *A narrow structure has not been allowed to restrict the choice of fireplace – it simply continues around the outside of the chimney-breast with a mirror hung above.*

Opposite: *A solid-fuel burning stove is often the answer to fireplace and chimney problems. This stove and its hood are unusually magnificent, but many modern stoves are handsome, especially when backed with coloured ceramic tiles.*

practical terms, decorative or mirrored freestanding firescreens look attractive placed in front of an empty grate in summer. Victorian ones are often embroidered, and hand-painted ones are also to be found. Alternatively, a flowering plant or a simple paper fan is an attractive way of giving some interest to the empty grate in summer.

A dilapidated, damaged or plain dull chimney-piece, which would otherwise not bear up to the attention which a fireplace inevitably attracts, can be rescued from obscurity by painting it with pictures or patterns. Chimney-pieces, fireplace lintels, linings and firebacks have been decorated for as long as man has built chimney-surrounds. Carving, paintings and cast-iron panels have portrayed, often in colour, all types of geometric shapes, intertwined lines, symbols, words and figurative scenes. A family living in the

country could paint (or have painted) a picture of themselves, their home and the surrounding landscape on the lintel.

A fire-surround in perfect condition, however, does not need cosmetic treatment. An elegant bow-fronted French marble fireplace, for example, should simply have a single magnificent mirror hung above it and a few appropriate objects arrayed on its mantelpiece.

The mantelpiece is almost as important a focus as the fireplace, being the part most nearly at eye level. It can be crowded with objects, or not, as taste dictates. A single object will attract a great deal of attention, so this is the perfect place to put a fine clock or family heirloom. The opposite effect can be equally appealing: a mass of accumulated bits and pieces such as postcards, pebbles and fir-cones collected on country walks, yellowing newspaper cuttings held down by a candlestick holding a dribbling candle, and old jugs and objects of sentimental value. The mantelpiece is an ideally isolated spot for some picturesquely calculated chaos.

If an open fire is not appropriate, another option for a fireplace is the cast-iron stove, either a woodburning or multi-fuel variety. The stove has been rediscovered as being practical, highly efficient in terms of heat production and attractive. Manufacturers now make a bewildering range in dozens of sizes, shapes, colours and styles. If the business of transporting logs, coal and ash does not appeal to you, it is possible to have a gas-fired stove. These work along the same lines as the real-flame, gas-powered open fires popular with town and apartment dwellers. The chimney recess behind a stove can be covered with plain or decorated tiles, painted cement render or any other heat-bearing material.

RADIATORS

While decorators practise their beautifying arts on the fire-surround, they also spend time thinking of new ways to hide or disguise the radiator. The simplest way to conceal a radiator is to camouflage it by painting it the same colour as the wall. If the wall is patterned, a painted approximation to the pattern can be successful, depending on the scale of the pattern and the skill and patience of the painter. If the pattern is small, the radiator will blend in if it is simply painted the same colour that the overall pattern on the wall gives when viewed from a distance, rather than any one of its constituent colours.

Another alternative is to box a radiator in. The cover should not look apologetic and, in a room with antique furniture, it should be properly finished, perhaps with beading and an architrave around the top. In a modern setting the casing can be simpler. There needs to be room for the air to circulate inside the box, otherwise the heating properties of the radiator will be entirely lost. The front of a radiator cover is a grille through which the heat can escape, usually formed from metal or wire mesh or painted, criss-crossed strips of wood. A compromise between boxing in a radiator and leaving it exposed is to build a shelf above it, upon which can be placed objects that will distract attention from the radiator. A radiator box can, of course, also be used rather like a mini-mantelpiece as a place to display objects.

Above: Antique, cast-iron radiators can be rescued from architectural reclamation yards. They have a solid, sculptural quality and fit well into modern interiors.

Opposite: Two pairs of objects and a single vase of flowers fill a mantelshelf. The effect of the deep colours and no-nonsense symmetrical arrangement, with the tall plants in matching cache-pots on the outside, is essentially masculine.

Radical alternatives to disguising the modern radiator are to do away with it, or to draw attention to it. In the former case, it can be replaced with a freestanding, cast-iron model of the type still to be seen in some elderly boarding schools and other institutions. These take up more room and are generally less efficient than modern radiators but have a solid, stately appearance, and can still be found in architectural reclamation yards. Modern radiators designed to be looked at rather than hidden away are made in dozens of colours and many geometric forms. Some are constructed as a long 'X' and others rise up the wall in a tall column, sometimes in the form of horizontal bars. The latter is especially useful in a bathroom, where the periodic gaps between the bars create an elegant and useful heated towel rail.

FURNISHING FABRICS

'So, although fabrics have a well-defined practical job to do in the home, their decorative function is even more important.'

Roger Smithells
Fabrics in the Home 1950

The acquisition of furniture involves choosing between different types and styles of finished object, which allows you to be discerning but offers little scope for creativity. Successful use of furnishing fabric in a room, however, makes very different demands. The challenge here is to put together a collection of colours, patterns and finishes, either from scratch or by drawing together existing soft furnishings, that will make a cohesive whole. Fabrics have to be considered in the context of wall, window, ceiling and floor colour and decoration. Overall, they must not only be consistent with each other visually, and with the furniture which they dress, but their character must create the atmosphere you want. Individually they should be attractive and appropriate to their use. The task of co-ordinating many different fabrics in a room is not easy, but it can be achieved more readily with imagination than it can with mere cash.

The cost of fabrics cannot, unfortunately, be dismissed entirely. Many of the most beautiful materials are ▶

Opposite: *The plain simple walls and floor in this room allow a long and heavy black damask tablecloth, which completely covers the table, to be dramatic without being at all overpowering.*
Right: *Cushions can be any shape. Here, the ornate cord piping and large tassel on a satin-covered cylinder emphasize a sofa's rich elegance.*

Left: *The designer of this room is particularly gifted with pattern, using five different rose-and-cream fabrics, including two checks, a stripe and a toile de Jouy, without the effect being fussy.*

Opposite: *For a candlelit winter feast the covers can be removed from these chairs to reveal their dark, gleaming wood. Meanwhile, their summery pale linen covers protect them from the sun.*

the material, and you would soon tire of it. The eye wants variety and stimulation, not monotony. On the other hand, a single fabric used cleverly can draw together disparate elements in a room or provide a unifying background for furniture already covered in a variety of patterns or colours.

On a piece of fabric-covered furniture such as a sofa or armchair, a plain colour can be given definition and an assertive pattern restrained by some judicious detailing. A sofa covered in a cheerful plaid loose cover, for instance, will be given a solid base by a deep twisted fringe laid over the hem to a depth of 10–15 cm (4–6 in). Piping made in a contrasting colour, or from a patterned fabric, gives a certain sharpness to the outlines of upholstery. Tassels give a touch of whimsy to furniture of heavy design. Braid is an elegant finishing touch along edges where fabric and woodwork meet, or along outside seams (bear in mind that it may not be comfortable to sit on). Cord can sometimes be used in the same way and given a looped twist at corners.

LOOSE COVERS

The great charm of loose covers is that they can be changed to create different moods or to alter the appearance of the furniture itself. A sofa that envelops you in warm woollen tartan in winter can become a rose-covered couch on which to lounge in summer. Empire-striped armchairs that in spring are fresh blue-and-white can be converted to cosy russet in autumn. The simplest cream calico cover, loose almost to the point of shapelessness, can transform a heavy William IV sofa into an airy confection which looks light enough to float away. High-backed dining chairs, whose polished wood looks so handsome by candlelight, can be both protected from sunshine and transformed by loose patterned covers with skirts, full or tailored, falling to the floor. These covers can be decorated with ties,

also the most expensive. Where the quality is superb, they can be looked upon as an investment, but many fabrics of good quality are not prohibitively expensive and can be backed-up with inexpensive, simple materials that will lower the overall outlay. Whatever the budget, fabric should be chosen slowly. It is easy to change the colour of plain painted walls if they are not right, but you may have to live with fabric mistakes for years.

Researching fabrics can be fun. Examine the current, and past, issues of the good-quality interior-decorating magazines. Explore your local interior-decorating shops and markets. Make mental notes when in other people's homes, including houses open to the public. Visit the showrooms of reputable fabric manufacturers and ask for small samples of materials that you like. Pin up samples of the fabrics you think you want to use, side by side on the wall, and look at them regularly in natural and artificial lights and at different times of day, before making a final decision. Fabric companies will often lend or hire a larger piece of their fabric to help you envisage it covering your sofas, chairs, window-seats or hanging at your windows.

As a starting point for choosing fabric, pinpoint two appropriate colours for a room, one dominant and one subordinate: rose red and

cream, for example, or strong blue and palest yellow, or terracotta and pale grey. With these in mind (and not necessarily excluding elements of other colours), gather a variety of fabrics of different pattern and weight. A lively selection might include a boldly patterned chintz or cotton, a plain linen union, a self-patterned Jacquard, a fresh and simple stripe, a cotton plaid or check, a tartan, a velvet, a sophisticated toile de Jouy, a silk brocade and even a tapestry. Match some of these fabrics to the articles they might cover, and perhaps pin them on them. Move them around now and then until you have chosen a core of three or four designs for each room.

In a drawing room, for instance, you might choose one fabric for the sofa, one for armchairs, one for curtains and tablecloths and one for window-seats or stools. A bedroom would need one fabric for a bed valance, one for a bed cover, one for curtains and perhaps one for chairs or stools or a dressing table. A fabric that you love but that does not seem to fit into this scheme, or which is too expensive, can be bought in a small quantity and used to cover cushions or a footstool. However, if you can afford the fabric of your dreams, beware of over-exposing it in a single room – the effect could be stunning but is more likely to be either bland or overwhelming, depending on

bows or rosettes. Some of the fuller ones whose swathes of fabric are bloused and gathered and constructed into folds look like discarded ballgowns. A more dignified restraint can be achieved by decorating chair covers with piping, twisted or tufted braid, or by simply leaving them unadorned.

CUSHIONS

Cushions give a rare opportunity to let the imagination run riot without enormous financial outlay. Their practical function is to increase the comfort of sofas and chairs. Visually, they offer endless decorative possibilities. Plain-coloured cushions can blend in with the fabric covering the piece of furniture, accent a particular colour or colours, or create a vibrant contrast – black-and-white cushions on a scarlet sofa, for example. Among the most attractive patterned cushions are those made from pieces of kelim or antique fabric; those with pictures and motifs painted, printed or appliquéd on them; embroidered cushions; and cushions made from patterned fabric. Different types of cushions can help create particular atmospheres: in the right setting, cushions made from fake fur or decorated with heraldic symbols add a touch of humour; antique embroidered cushions backed with softly faded velvet give a sophisticated traditional feel; those with handpainted decoration lend an air of high bohemianism, and cushions printed with classical architectural motifs suggest restrained elegance.

Cushions are another decorative item that can be changed with the seasons. Summer's cheerful yellow cotton cover can be unzipped and removed, to be replaced by winter's more melancholy greens, blues and browns. Or the winter months could be enlivened by vibrant colours after a summer of romantically faded tones. Variety can come from shape as much as from colour and decoration. Circular cushions are as comfortable as square or rec-

Above right: *Cushions on the settee are covered in the same elegant fabric as the seats of the chairs alongside, linking them together, while the settee has a fabric which is similar but without the stripes.*

Right: *A mosquito net suspended over a cushion-covered sofa is an ethereal canopy which transforms the sofa into an oasis of repose and romance. Once inside, the gauze walls will put the world at one remove.*

tangular ones. The recent burgeoning of popular enthusiasm for figurative canvas work has resulted in cushions the shape of the subject depicted, such as a curled-up cat. With a little initiative and imagination it is possible to create your own cushion decorations, if not with embroidery wool then with a sewing-machine or fabric paints.

The character of a cleverly decorated room will be revealed and encapsulated as much by the way the cushions are arranged on a sofa or window-seat as by the covers themselves. They can be neatly stacked up in the corners, arranged with some precision along the length of the seat or scattered with abandon over the furniture and even the floor, giving an exotic and relaxed impression. However they are distributed, they should always be well plumped-up. Sad, flattened cushions are not inviting or comfortable.

In a small home where the furniture needs to be as versatile as possible, cushions are an enormous asset. A thick, comfortable cushion made to fit a small and sturdy low modern table, for example, will transform it into extra seating at a moment's notice. Deck chairs make excellent budget armchairs or extra seating and are easier to get up from (as well as being more comfortable) if the bottom of the loose canvas seat is filled with a big squashy cushion. Wooden or metal fold-up garden chairs make useful and stylish emergency seating but, if you have to remain seated on one for the length of a dinner party, you may wish it had a cushion.

Wooden and rush-seated dining or kitchen chairs are made more comfortable by neat cushions that fit the seat shape and tie on at the back. Seat cushions also provide a way of introducing extra colour to a room or of altering its character. In a kitchen-dining room, for example, the chairs could have brightly-coloured gingham cushions for everyday use, and cushions (or covers) made

Above left: *A pair of elegant day beds, placed each side of a fireplace, are covered in white with black piping to give them definition. Black-and-white striped cushions give a lift to this ultra-restrained scheme.*

Left: *A comfortable, squashy sofa has grey covers piped in yellow – the same colour as the walls. Antique cushions make the sofa even more inviting. Tables alongside have heavy cloths which drape on the floor.*

from a more sophisticated fabric in a different colour for special occasions. The everyday cushions could be attached to the chairs with utilitarian string-ribbons or stud fasteners, and the special cushions with a full fabric bow, rosette or tassel-ended cord. Whatever the fastening, it needs to be strong and securely attached to the cushion or cover, which should in turn be reinforced at the meeting point. Seat cushions are notorious for coming adrift from their chair fastenings, because the slightest movement by the person sitting in the chair strains them.

Window-seat cushions usually stay put without any fastening, but if recalcitrant they could be secured with Velcro, one side of which is glued to the wooden seat. The cushions usually take the form of flat squabs or thicker boxed cushions, shaped to fit the seat. A fabric that corresponds with the window curtains, but is not identical to it, is a subtle choice for covering window-seat cushions and will not dissipate the impact made by the curtains. The addition of smaller cushions of varied colour and pattern can render the seat more comfortable and visually interesting.

Above: A jumble of cushions and covers of different patterns are drawn together by a red/pink colour theme. An antique shawl is thrown over the back of the sofa and an antique hatbox is used as a table.

Opposite right: All kinds of textiles can be used as table covers, including carpets. Here, warmly coloured rugs protect the table beneath and provide a background for a display of antique objects.

THROWOVERS AND TABLE COVERINGS

One of the easiest ways to alter the appearance of a sofa or chair is by throwing a shawl, quilt or rug over it. The more beautiful the shawl, the more dramatic the transformation – embroidered or printed silks and Paisley wool are particularly effective. Also useful as throwovers are the light woollen rugs designated as 'throws' by manufacturers, which also double as shawls or blankets. A tartan rug will make a sofa look comfortable and welcoming.

Rugs and carpets have been used as table covers since the seventeenth century and

before, when they were sometimes part of a suite of hangings, commissioned for a specific room. A small kelim or a picnic rug makes a luxurious table covering and one which will give the table beneath greater protection than a lighter fabric. A heavy fabric is preferable for covering a cheap, self-assembly table; such tables are coarsely made and any rough edges will be better disguised by a thick tablecloth. Gauze can in turn be laid over a kelim or other carpet to protect it.

A dining table that is frequently used can be protected by a thick heavy under-cloth made from linen union or coarse silk, perhaps supported by a cotton lining, that falls to or drapes on to the floor. A cotton or other everyday tablecloth can be placed over this. If the under-cloth is of a rich or deep colour, a fine semi-transparent table-cloth incorporating drawn-thread work or lace will create a splendid, but not strictly practical, cover. More magnificent and aristocratic, however, would be a huge, stiff damask cloth falling in conical points at the table's corners and accompanied by generous snow-white damask table napkins.

*An elaborate chair treatment has cushions
for backs as well as seats, and the seat
cushions have a valance covering the tops of
legs (top). A simpler solution is an over-all
loose cover (centre). Kitchen chairs can be
smartened up with colourful flat squab
cushions, securely fastened (bottom).*

LIGHTING

Natural light alters the appearance of everything it touches: a clear-cut image seen in early morning light can become a hazy golden mirage at noon and a blue-grey ghost at dusk. Throughout history the physical qualities of light have fascinated man, and writers and painters have striven to capture its changeable beauty. Today, artificial lighting is so versatile it can be used to reproduce many of the effects created by natural light. The mood and appearance of any room can be transformed with a flick of the switch.

The business of choosing lighting involves deciding what effect you want to achieve with what type of fixtures. Because of the technical nature of electrical lighting systems, the outlines of a scheme have to be thought out long before the finishing touches stage. New wiring, power points, transformers and dimmer switches may be required and a lighting expert or electrician needs to install these before you decorate. If you dislike central pendant lights, for instance, or if the ceilings of your home are too low for ▶

Left: *Candles provide soft warm light. This elegant sconce in the shape of a leaf is gilded and has other leaves, dried, carelessly attached to it with a satin ribbon. The combined effect is subdued, simple and poetic.*
Right: *A pleasant but ordinary table lamp is transformed by being swathed in layers of translucent net tied in a knot at the top.*

them, power will need to be run to extra points in the walls, and possibly the floor, to supply wall brackets and lamps. But once the technical requirements are satisfied, lighting possibilities for your home are as varied and exciting as are sweets for children.

Overall, the best lighting scheme is one that offers maximum choice. A switch at the door is needed to provide light to get you into the room, after which you should be able to give the room a bright, energetic look or a subdued, cosy appearance, according to its function or the occasion. In a bedroom, for example, overall light enables you to see clearly into wardrobes and drawers and assess your appearance in a mirror. When it comes to reading in bed, however, this amount of light is unnecessary and probably not well-enough directed. Bedside lamps are what is wanted.

OVERHEAD LIGHTING

Perhaps the most elegant pendant ceiling light of all is the chandelier, popular for several centuries. The most romantic and beautiful of these are formed from a cascade of crystal drops, which playfully reflect and refract the light that passes through them. If the light is supplied by candles rather than electric light bulbs, the effect is subtle (though you should beware of spilt wax when standing underneath). Chandeliers have been made from crystal and clear glass since the seventeenth century, but they are also constructed from other materials. Coloured glass ones have a more arcadian appearance; brass or metal chandeliers of seventeenth-century design

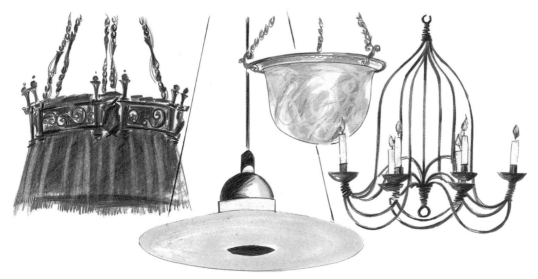

Above left: Candlelight instantly conjures up an atmosphere, here reflecting off dark wood furniture and pale walls. The curtainless window with shutters, tartan rug used as a table-cloth, textile wall-hanging and brick floor all contribute to the mood.

Opposite: As dusk falls, fading natural daylight is supplemented by a magnificent chandelier, candles on table and window-sill, and a pair of table lamps.

Pendant ceiling fitments come in a variety of traditional and modern styles including the hanging candelabrum, the Arts and Crafts style belt complete with fabric shade, the hanging bowl and the Castiglioni 'Frisbi'.

suit a more ascetic interior, as do chandeliers in a modern style. Old wooden, carved and gilded chandeliers of simple construction with few arms are quite easy to find in local antique shops and markets, as are other types of antique light fitments.

An important consideration when choosing a chandelier is scale. Not all private homes have rooms of the right dimensions for a large chandelier. The ceiling has to be of more than average height and the period and proportions of the room appropriate to a device of such sophisticated and intricate appearance. A branched monster half-filling a terrace sitting room could be a dramatic part of an interior intended to be surreal, but in general it would be as much out of place as a pretty gilt spider marooned high above a ballroom. But

not all chandeliers are gargantuan, and the years are long gone when revellers ran the risk of snagging their tall powdered wigs on the lighting apparatus if it was hung too low. A stairwell or hallway might be the most receptive space for a chandelier, if its size or formality is unsuitable elsewhere.

The hanging candelabrum is a type of chandelier in which the light comes not from electric bulbs but from candles. For the full effect to be appreciated, it should be in a place such as a dining room, where it is not necessary that the light be terrifically bright – somewhere, in fact, where the subdued light is a virtue. A hanging candelabrum can obviously be supplemented with electric light from lamps placed elsewhere in the room, but this should be subtle so that the candles

appear to be the main source of light.

The difference between lighting a dining room and lighting any other room is that the priorities are to some extent reversed. Elsewhere the aim may be to provide general light, perhaps focusing on a selection of pictures or objects and bright enough in some places to read by. In a dining room, however, the ideal is light that is not general but particular, lighting the table and the people around it. There's no worse start to a meal, as visitors to the red-light-and-Muzak school of restaurant well know, than not being able to see properly what you are eating. Candles and candelabra are an obvious and elegant solution to this problem, but there are others.

A modern hanging lamp of good design would be suitable for a modern dining room.

Nineteenth- and early twentieth-century hanging lamps can still be found in a variety of remarkable designs, including a type of Arts and Crafts brass belt that takes about three bulbs. Between the patterned brass belt and the bayonet bulb fittings inside you can insert a skirt of gathered fabric which hangs down below the rim and softens the light – this looks effective over a table in a room decorated in a traditional style. Nineteenth-century adjustable hanging lamps had magnificent brass and china counterbalances which, when in good condition, work just as well today as they did when new. The type of modern pendant lamp that can be raised and lowered on a spring is useful in a kitchen or utilitarian dining room. For best effect a hanging lamp should be hung so that it is just above the height of your head when you are seated at the table.

Other modern forms of overhead lighting can be successful when combined with candlelight. One such is a low-voltage halogen fitment recessed into the ceiling and controlled by a dimmer switch. Such lights are available in many different sizes, and if you have a ceiling rose (medallion), a small one could be sunk discreetly into that. Halogen bulbs produce light that is much whiter than that produced by ordinary lightbulbs and is therefore much nearer the quality of natural light. When dimmed the light is soft – somewhat like

Above left: Downlighters recessed into the ceiling are amongst the most discreet modern fitments. Several together can give a good overall light which will here reflect off pale walls and the white tiled floor.

Above right: In any working area, daylight is the ideal form of lighting. Blinds diffuse the strong midday sun and are more hygienic than curtains. Electric light is supplied by adjustable overhead spots on a track.

Opposite: Different forms of lighting work quietly together as a team. Classic silver candlesticks contrast with a tall modern matt black standard lamp and light diffused by a simple oriental paper screen.

candlelight. The low-voltage filament is a fraction of the size of a normal bulb's, so fittings can be very small and neat. Perhaps the most romantic type of low-voltage light is the smallest – the star light. These are tiny bulbs, a number of which, inserted through the ceiling from above, look magically like stars when lit.

Ordinary spotlights are eminently practical and versatile, but not usually elegant. Downlighters of all types, especially low-voltage ones, are a discreet way of lighting any room or space, since no fitting is visible. However,

there must be space between the ceiling and the floor above to accommodate the unseen workings of the light and, if necessary, a transformer. Recessed downlighters are especially practical in functional rooms such as kitchens and bathrooms where the emphasis is on clean lines, hygiene and good illumination, and for which the design of practical lighting fitments is, in general, less than inspiring.

TABLE AND FLOOR-STANDING LAMPS

Other traditional types of lighting fitment are wall brackets, standard or floor-standing lamps and table lamps. Here the difficulty is not limited choice but an *embarras de richesse*. A decision should of course be guided by the room's main decorations and the question of practicality. The ideal arrangement gives good light where it is wanted without the lamps being too bright, too numerous, too large or too small. Small lamps look mean or apologetic unless their scale is in keeping with their surroundings. Large lamps are luxurious and look as if you are not embarrassed by them – indeed, they contribute to the overall decorative statement.

Standard lamps provide good reading light and can be placed anywhere in a room, not just where there happens to be a side table. However it is much harder to find an elegant standard lamp than a table lamp.

It is vital to have the right shade for a lamp, in terms of shape, size and material. If in doubt as to what size and style of shade to buy, err on the side of simplicity and generosity – shades should be of sufficient size to prevent any danger or singeing.

Among the most interesting table lamps are those not originally designed for that use. Vases made of everything from terracotta to porcelain, eighteenth-century medicine jars and ornate wooden or brass candlesticks can all be converted into lamps. Pairs and sets of table lamps are especially useful since they can be the basis for a symmetrical arrangement around a fireplace or either side of a piece of furniture such as a sofa. They also provide a link between the different parts of the room where they are placed.

The opposite of the downlighter in terms of the direction of the light emitted is the uplighter. These can be bought or easily

Above left: Precious china and glass is safe and handsomely displayed in a glass-fronted, built-in cabinet with its own interior lighting. The cabinet is cleverly incorporated into the room's blue-and-cream colour scheme.

Above right: Black is the link between a pair of elaborate candelabra and a geometric arrangement of modern pictures. The candlelight is supplemented by a hidden spot which shines on the pictures from above.

Opposite top: Pairs of lamps are especially useful and look their best placed symmetrically. Here, they create twin pools of light which illuminate architectural prints attached directly to the wall.

made (for a more rugged look) and stand on the floor or on a table. From there they cast light upwards in a column, illuminating anything that is in the way such as plants and pictures. Uplighters generally sit discreetly out of sight on the floor.

CANDLELIGHT

The gentle glowing light generated by candles is flattering and seductive. It hovers and flickers in a most alluring way. (When electric light began to be introduced at dinner tables in the nineteenth century, it was hardly surprising that ladies often complained that it was too bright and hard and did nothing for the appearance of their complexions.)

A passion for candlelight is easily aroused, and there is nothing to stop you lighting entire rooms with it, using combinations of hanging and standing candelabra, candlesticks and light brackets that have not been converted to

electricity. Light brackets complete with mirrored sconces would be particularly useful.

Mirrors hung in a candlelit room increase the amount of light if they catch the reflections of the flickering flames, and may remove the necessity for supplementary electric lamps altogether. An alternative is to put a standing candelabrum or candlesticks on a mirror placed under them on the table, creating a reflected pool of light.

Candle shades can be bought made from either fabric or paper attached to a metal frame that sits on the top of the lit candle. It is important to take fire hazards into account when positioning candles.

SWITCHES

A light switch does not have to be the square white plastic block supplied as standard. Brass, chrome and burnished 'antique' bronze are among the alternatives, as are

Light switches made of wood, brass and marbled plastic are available in many styles.

dolly switches. On these, the switch that you flick is a toggle rather than a panel and gives a pleasantly solid sound when flipped up or down. Dolly switches have an old-fashioned appearance but they too are made in a range of materials including wood and clear glass or plastic. The latter is unobtrusive since the paint or wallpaper continues under the plate and is seen through the glass. The toggle is the only part of the switch that shows.

Ordinary white plastic switches can be concealed in a number of ways. They can be covered with the paper that covers the walls; this is usually done when the room is decorated. Alternatively, they can be hidden in a box or recess behind a small door.

A simple dimmer switch can be used to achieve a similar but less romantic effect to that created by a candlelit room. Although it is easily installed, it cannot be used with all types of electric fitment.

OCCASIONAL FURNITURE

'A wise discrimination is necessary, not only in the quality but the quantity of furniture that is placed in the room.'

Joseph Crouch and Edmund Butler
The Apartments of the House 1900

Left: *The pier or wall between two windows has traditionally been the place for a table with a mirror – pier glass – or, as here, pictures hung above. Note also the neat radiator covers, fitted each side of the table.*
Right: *A modern variation in brass and glass of the whatnot, a tiered side table for display, is here loaded with a pot collection.*

Large pieces of furniture such as chests of drawers, dining tables and sofas tend to be purchased after long and careful consideration. They provide the basic structure for a room's furnishings, defining its use and dividing its space. Smaller pieces of occasional furniture add detail to this bold outline and need not involve such great financial outlay. As well as being interesting visually, they fulfil a great variety of invaluable practical functions.

The most necessary piece of small furniture is the occasional table, and this is especially true in a drawing room or living room. Sofas and chairs need tables near them upon which to put lamps, cups of tea or drinks, small boxes and objects, books and magazines. Pairs of matching tables are particularly useful and are seen to best effect in a symmetrical arrangement with one at each side of a sofa or fireplace. A large room can sometimes take two pairs of tables, at the ends of two sofas for example, but in a smaller room too many identical tables are undoubtedly monotonous. The ideal is ▶

Left: *Hanging cupboards provide useful storage space, both inside and on top, which can be taken with you when you move. Small decorative ones like these are especially good for rooms with collections of bottles and jars.*

Opposite: *Almost anything with a flat top can be converted into an occasional table, including boxes and trunks like this magnificent oriental red lacquer example.*

a variety of small tables of different designs, each of which fulfils a particular function. For this reason it is worth giving some attention to their height, so that a side table is not too far below or above the arm of a chair or sofa. Tables can also be placed so that they become the focus in an otherwise vacant space. A round table with objects upon it, placed in the centre of a spacious but dull hallway or stairwell, will, for example, provide interest and make the area less uninviting.

Finding the perfect pair of side tables may be an expensive business, especially if you want antiques. There are, however, many types to choose from and examples from the nineteenth century, when display of possessions was almost a mania, include such diverse styles as carved Gothic, Arts and Crafts and bamboo. If you want to take a cheap short cut, you can buy two mass-produced tables and cover them with identical cloths, edged with cord or braid and reaching generously to the floor. Alternatively, the tables can be painted in a finish appropriate to the room's decorations and left uncovered.

All kinds of objects can be used as side tables as long as they offer a stable and level

Mass-produced tables made from inexpensive wood or chipboard (particleboard) make useful side tables.

surface. A lacquer-covered oriental trunk, an old-fashioned trunk, a blanket box or ancient carved chest – any of these will suffice, so long as access to objects stored in them is not needed regularly. A decorative panel of any material such as carved and painted wood, lacquer or tooled leather can be converted into a small table: a cradle has to be made for it by a joiner and protective glass placed over the panel. Ordinary-looking tables are transformed with the aid of a sheet of glass, under which can be placed a map of the area, photographs, the covers of past issues of decorative magazines or any collage of paper matter, which can be changed from time to time. An outrageous Casanova could display his love letters and a wine-lover his most decorative labels.

Whatnots and trolleys are types of table with particular versatility. Both offer several surfaces on which to put things, and the trolley can be moved about. The whatnot is another product of the Victorian love of displaying possessions. It generally consists of three or more shelves supported by a post at each corner and was designed to be placed against a wall. The top layer can be used like any other table surface, especially if the whatnot is doubling as a bedside table beside a high bed. Books or decorative objects can be arranged on the lower layers. Triangular corner whatnots help create interest in what can be an empty part of a room.

An invaluable piece of small furniture that can be used as a table – although not designed for that purpose – is the stool. Stools were a common form of seating when the possession of a chair was still a status symbol and they have survived in quantity in every style and from every period since the sixteenth century. They are also extremely popular on account of their versatility: stools used as tables can easily revert to seating as occasion demands. Collectors of early furniture favour

seventeenth-century oak joint stools as side tables, while nineteenth-century ones with turned legs are unpretentious, adaptable and less expensive. Upholstered stools are not suitable for putting lamps and glasses on but can be piled up with books and periodicals. Long upholstered stools are particularly useful in a hall or passage where there is not enough space for a bulkier piece of furniture,· and at the foot of a bed.

The nineteenth century was the heyday of the footstool; today footstools are kept more for their decorative than their practical value, although they are none the less extremely comfortable and relaxing to use. Mid-Victorian footstools are frequently upholstered with their original Berlin wool work, a type of canvas stitched with special coloured wools, depicting flowers. Footstools covered with antique needlework or textile are worth protecting with a simple cover, made from linen or other suitable fabric, that can be removed for special occasions.

Another useful type of small furniture is the stand. The word is used to describe a piece designed as a support or a container – the most familiar being the coat stand and umbrella stand found in a hallway. Any container of suitable size and weight can be used as an umbrella stand, although only a purpose-made one will have a removable tray at the bottom for collecting water from damp umbrellas. Small stands made from brass, other metals or wood are the neatest and smartest in a confined space.

Jardinières and torchères provide a way of bringing plant life into the house without cluttering up tables and window sills. The jardinière's name comes from the fact that it was specifically designed to hold a plant. It is a short or tall stand formed from a stalk and a bowl or basket, which are separate, and it is generally made from wood, china or cast iron. The torchère is a narrow stand with a flat top

Right top: *An unusual piece of furniture like this octagonal table will be a centre-piece in a hall or stairwell. Positioned at the bottom of stairs it acts as a visual flourish to the descending line of the balustrade.*

Right bottom: *A large and handsome whatnot can be used for storage of attractive objects (here, baskets and an oyster dish) as well as for display. Note also the richly marbled skirting where walls and floor meet.*

like a small round table at shoulder height and was designed (as its name suggests) as a stand for a lamp or candelabrum. At this height, the light could be directed better and the area upon which it fell was increased. A torchère can be used for this purpose or as a stand for anything that will safely fit on it, such as a plant in a cache-pot, flowers in a vase, a decorative object or a sculpture.

Plinths and pedestals designed specifically for displaying objects and sculpture should be sympathetic to the object itself and discreet in style, rather than flamboyant, lest they become distractions. A polished or marbled wooden column of bold, simple style, such as the classical Ionic order, makes a handsome pedestal, and tapering, square, perspex (plexiglass) pedestals are well suited to modern sculpture.

The magazine rack is a useful way of gathering the month's periodicals together tidily, unless you prefer to have them on display on a table or stool. An eighteenth- or nineteenth-century Canterbury, which was designed to hold books of music, will double as a magazine rack. The Canterbury was a divided rack with a drawer beneath for loose sheet music and was usually mounted on castors so it could be pushed under the grand piano.

The panel screen is extremely versatile and can do the work of various other articles. It can replace a door or provide draught-proofing in front of it, and it can be drawn across a window in place of curtains. In a bedroom, a screen can shield a hand basin from sight and in any room it can be used as a divider, separating areas with different functions. Traditionally the screen has been made from a wide variety of materials including leather, carved and gilded wood and glass, and lacquered oriental panels. Victorian scrap screens are among the most intriguing, while modern screens are often the boldest in form and decoration.

Left top: *Lurking between a big squashy armchair and a marble and metal occasional table is a small stool doubling as a telephone table. Stools of every kind are versatile and invaluable.*

Left bottom: *Folding furniture like this table can be brought out when needed. Decorative screens have a wide range of uses – in doorways, at windows or hiding unsightly clutter in the corner of a room.*

DISPLAY

'... the Elegance of that Room is
from the lightness of well-disposed,
well-executed Ornaments.'

Lord Melbourne
1774

The display of treasured possessions, collections, decorative ephemera and household objects reveals a great deal about a person's interests and character. These things also contribute greatly to the appearance a room has of being lived in and enjoyed – a signal, as it were, of a healthy relationship between a home and its inhabitants. People have always used their possessions to define their position in society as they would like it to be seen. In Western society a healthy display of silver and porcelain was for centuries an important status symbol and one which the newly rich would buy at the first opportunity. On an aesthetic level, the contemplation of well-formed objects – whatever their value – is a pleasure open to everybody. These objects need not be rare and precious – kitchen pans and everyday china of interesting design or decoration are as worthy of display in appropriate surroundings as the greatest Sèvres dinner service.

Most households have a quantity of china and glass for practical ►

Left: *Sparkling glass looks magnificent set against richly polished dark wood. It looks especially good when massed but then separated in the splendid isolation which this intriguing cabinet's compartments give to each piece.*
Right: *Lightweight objects such as baskets can be crowded together on walls for a rich and varied textural effect.*

purposes. The china on show may be the best pieces (perhaps acquired specifically for display rather than use), those in excess of daily requirements or just attractive ordinary china. Fine china should be displayed in a protective cabinet, preferably behind glass, whereas less valuable china can be more versatile in its use for display. It can decorate the walls of kitchens and bathrooms, rooms which tend to be steamy and are not therefore ideal environments for all types of picture. The wall against which the stove or hob is placed gets damp and greasy and is not suitable for storage of implements or food. A single large dish or arrangement of smaller plates will decorate the wall and can easily be wiped clean.

Plates are one of the most useful types of china for display on furniture, in cabinets or on walls, and a pretty but broken plate can be mended for display though not for the ravages of renewed use. Plates can be laid flat on a surface where they can be seen from above but are not likely to have other objects placed on them. They can be raised above the surface, to make it clear that they are on display, by being placed on round carved wooden stands. If displayed in cabinets or on tables, they can be tipped up on a wire or wooden stand so that the decoration can readily be seen and, if they are on a dresser, they are propped up behind a strip of beading or a groove incorporated into the structure of the shelf. Plates displayed on walls are hung either from a plastic-covered wire frame, which grips the plate at points around its circumference, or from a loop attached to a disc which is stuck to the back of the plate (and can be removed when necessary by soaking for a few hours in water).

Some thought needs to be given to the arrangement of a group of plates. A collection of different single plates can be linked by a theme, such as botanical decoration or colour, to make a cohesive display. Plates can be hung in any room, not only in a kitchen or bathroom. A set of pretty dessert plates decorated with fruit or birds is appropriate in a drawing room; a set with hunting scenes is handsome in a study. They are best grouped together or hung up the sides of a largish picture or mirror,

Right: *The sheer number and variety of objects in this astonishing display of white and cream china on a white dresser makes an impact. The fact that the pieces are all white and cream pulls them together.*

Right: *A shelf running around a room at head height provides storage space and a display of decorative earthenware crockery. Display of everyday china and implements continues below.*

Below: *A window uncluttered with curtains or blinds is the setting for a play of colours and geometric shapes. Glass plates look stunning with light shining through them, and their circles cut across the panes.*

or positioned in a line near the top of the wall, in order to give their relatively small size some visual support.

Jugs and teapots are perhaps the most varied and interesting types of china in form and decoration. Plain jugs of fine colour, jugs decorated with handpainted flowers, transfers of picturesque views or splotchy Victorian lustreware, commemorative jugs, jugs of severely simple form, elaborate jugs – the possibilities are endless. The same is true of teapots. Objects of the same type make a greater impact when gathered together in one place rather than being dotted about a room, unless there are a great many of them. Teapots can be arranged in a row on a shelf, either all pointing in the same direction, or pointing in opposite directions towards the middle of the row. If your collection is all of the same size and shape, however, it is possible to create some variety and a focus by intro-

ducing another type of object, larger than the others but of compatible design. A collection of chrome and white Art Deco teapots could be arranged around a taller coffee pot or a clock of the same period, for example, with smaller milk jugs, sugar basins and egg cups in attendance.

Pairs of objects displayed on a shelf or mantelpiece make a greater impact if they are organized in a symmetrical arrangement, with another object between them acting as a focus and a contrast. Two blue-and-white vases of Chinese design could be placed either near the centre of a mantelpiece with a crystal bowl between them, or at the outer ends of the mantelpiece with other, smaller pairs of objects correspondingly arranged from the outside inwards, meeting at the crystal bowl in the centre. This arrangement of objects, especially of china, has been recognized as elegant and impressive for centuries.

Sets of three, five or seven pieces of china created specifically for display were popular in wealthy seventeenth-century homes and were known as garnitures. The set consisted of several pairs of matching jars or vases, with a single object to act as the centre-piece, and was prominently placed on a mantelshelf or, more rarely, on a projecting cornice (crown molding) over a door.

The alternative to a traditional symmetrical arrangement of a pair of objects is a strongly asymmetrical one, with the pair side by side at one end of a shelf. Greater visual skill and assurance is needed to make this succeed, but it can look fresh and dynamic. A single large picture or mirror hung above the objects (or, in the case of an overmantel mirror, hung behind them, reaching right down to the mantelpiece) will give the arrangement added impetus; whereas a collection of small pictures will probably distract attention from it.

Left: *A single bold object is displayed in a triangular niche by a door. The modernity of the pot and the setting, and the link between the stark white interior and the pot's white decorations make this a satisfying sight.*

Below: *The nook between a window frame and the corner of the room is filled with a series of small shelves for displaying flowers and blue china whose colour tones with the grey-blue paintwork.*

China and glass stored in a kitchen for everyday use can also make a visual display by being stacked in open-fronted cupboards or on shelves. Ideally these should be well away from steam-generating equipment (sink, cooker, dishwasher and so on) as they lack the protection from steam that cupboard doors provide. This arrangement also means china has to be kept in good order, or at least in some kind of order, or the decorative effect will be lost, as it will also if the space is over-crowded. Designs that look best displayed in this way are bold, fresh and simple.

Glass is an astonishing material and articles made from it can be incomparably beautiful. An array of sparkling glasses makes a dining table look magnificent and welcoming. Even quite mundane forms are transfigured when fashioned in glass, and a quantity of glass vessels of different shapes gathered in one place looks stunning. Light

HISTOIRE ANCIENNE
ANQUETIL HISTOIRE DE FRANCE
DON QUICHOTTE

shining through highly polished glass, especially crystal, gives it an almost ethereal beauty which is increased if it stands against a dark background. Traditional glass cabinets are often lined with navy blue or another dark-coloured velvet, which absorbs the light and throws the glass into relief. Engraved glass needs to be carefully lit, sometimes from above, for best effect.

A simple window can provide good back lighting for a display of glass on a table in front of it, on the window sill or on shelves (ideally made of glass) built into the recess created by the thickness of the wall. Coloured glass looks dramatic displayed in this way as the natural light gives its colour added luminosity, though the effect is lost after dark, of course. The corner whatnot (page 84) and the corner cupboard are useful pieces of furniture for displaying glass and china and creating interest in what can be a dull spot in a room. If a corner cupboard does not have glass panels in its doors, the contents can be displayed by opening the doors so that they lie back along the wall on each side.

MISCELLANEOUS OBJECTS

A glass-topped table with a velvet-lined tray beneath provides a charming way of displaying a collection of small precious articles such as glass paperweights, snuff boxes, silver toys and animals or fossils. The top lifts on

Above left: *A collection of baskets, wicker-covered bottles, flasks and jars takes its strength from the grouping of objects according to height, with the basket of foliage and berries adding variety.*

Above right: *Unsophisticated natural materials – earthenware and unpolished wood, dried flowers, grasses and wicker – form a still life with a couple of old hats.*

Opposite: *Massed rows of leather books make a fine display, but a break in their ranks can be welcome to the eye and the object or picture which interrupts them will be a focus for attention.*

hinges like the lid of a box and can usually be locked for security. The flat top of any piece of furniture, such as a bookcase, table or desk, can be used to display a regiment of family photographs or a single magnificent object. A desk is the obvious place to display desk furniture such as a blotter, ink well, pen tray, pencil drum and paper rack, but in lieu of a desk the same arrangement of these things can be made on a rectangular table. Collections of objects should, if possible, be displayed on a table or in a cabinet of roughly the same period, or a compatible one. Objects displayed on a side table or sofa table should

offer some variety of height and size or they may look monotonous. The ideal arrangement is one that combines structure with intrigue, tempting a visitor to approach and look at individual pieces more closely.

Books with particularly interesting or handsome covers can be laid on a round table. The contrast between the roundness of the table and the rectangular books lying end-on to the edge like spokes of a wheel is tremendously satisfying. An object placed in the middle of the table can add to the impact. Small pictures, too, can be displayed on tables, propped up on small stands or easels. One advantage of this arrangement is that they can be moved or changed with much less trouble than when hung on the wall.

An unconventional display of objects is one that spills from a table on to the floor beneath and perhaps on to a chair alongside, creating a large still life. A sculpture or large vase could be placed on the floor, and pictures propped up on the chair. The danger of this arrangement is that someone may kick or sit on your possessions – only you can assess the relative clumsiness of your family and friends. Some objects can be displayed by being hung directly on the wall. Hats, baskets, oriental shoes, miniature furniture, antique toys, wooden implements, and any other light-weight decorative objects can be grouped together to form an arresting and attractive

for ever. The advantage of free-standing
bookcases is that you can move them at a
later date, and you have a piece of furniture
that will probably increase in value. Which you
choose will also depend on the scale of your
home and the number of your books. A large
bookcase will look magnificent in a Georgian
house with high ceilings, whereas fitted shelving will make the best use of limited space in
a low-ceilinged cottage or small modern
house or apartment.

Book and display shelving can be used to
organize space, by dividing it or unifying it. In
a Victorian terrace house in which the two
ground-floor rooms have been knocked into
one long room, a bookcase or book shelving
filling the space between the two chimney-
breasts creates a link between the two halves
of the room, drawing them together. The
space between windows or a blank wall at the
end of a passage or bottom of a staircase can
be made more interesting by shelves filled
with books or objects, or a mixture of the two.
In a child's bedroom, shelves can be used for
storing toys and games – in this way they can
be found easily because they can be seen
and are always accessible.

In a small room or apartment, shelves can
be used to help create an illusion of space, if
the wall behind them is lined with mirror.
Objects displayed on the shelves will then
give the impression of merely screening a
greater space beyond. In places where the
flat end of a built-in bookcase or shelves will
look unattractive, the end can simply be left off
(so long as support can be provided in
another way) and the corners perhaps
rounded to improve their appearance and for
safety. In a house with sufficiently high ceilings, a single narrow shelf built around several
walls or an entire room, at shoulder height or
just below the level of a cornice, provides a
stunning method of displaying objects, especially glass, china and small pictures.

wall display. Brackets fixed to the wall provide
rather better support for objects that are too
precious or heavy to hang directly on the wall
but nonetheless worthy of prominent display.

BOOKS

A great many people would agree with the
nineteenth-century man of letters, the Rev.
Sidney Smith, that there is 'no furniture so
charming as books'. Collections of books tend
to grow with a life of their own and are housed
in shelves and bookcases installed here and
there around the house in whatever place
seems a good idea at the time. When you
decide on a major redecoration or move to a
new home or even simply think it is time for a
reorganization, that is the moment to decide
on a policy for books. From a practical point of
view, most of your books should be in one or
two places, which makes it easier to locate a
book when you want it. They also look more
magnificent in massed ranks, and act, in
quantity, as insulation.

Books are so attractive that it is natural to
want a few in every room, especially in your
bedroom where you want easy access to
much-read favourites and your current reading. Books in a spare bedroom make it more
welcoming, and cook books should obviously
be kept where they are needed – in the

kitchen. In these rooms smaller bookcases
are wanted, and their tops (if they are floor-
standing) can double as bedside tables or
places for display. A slim bookcase can be
recruited as a hall table, in a hall too small or
narrow for a table or other larger furniture.
Wall-mounted bookcases can be exceptionally pretty but can only be fixed to sturdy walls
because of the weight of books, but the load
can be lightened if a few objects are displayed as well as books. Very often such
bookcases incorporate small drawers or cupboards, which also help spread the weight.

SHELVING

The first decision to make before commission-
ing (or building or buying) display or book
shelving is whether to have free-standing or
fitted shelves. The advantage of fitted shelves
is that they make the maximum use of available space, filling a wall or recess to its edges.
They can run across the tops of doors, making
use of the space and (if notable objects are
placed on them here) adding interest to the
door; they can also put nooks and crannies to
work, in dark corners of rooms, under stairs
and between windows. The disadvantage is
that they cannot be taken with you when you
move, which is irrelevant if you have found the
house of your dreams and intend to stay put

FLOWERS
AND FOLIAGE

'Do we not always feel welcome when, on
entering a room, we find a display of
flowers on a table.'

Shirley Hibberd
Homes of Taste 1856

Flowers and plants give a house colour and life. Floral motifs have been used on fabrics and wallpapers since these decorative coverings first appeared. The greatest wallpaper designers, working in eighteenth-century France and late nineteenth-century Britain, used different types of flowers for entirely different effects but both were obviously attracted by the astonishing beauty, complexity of form and variety of colour created by nature.

It is only natural to want to fill your home with flowers and foliage, especially

Left: *Tulips that once were stiffly upright like sentries have matured into a still life as fine as any painting. Modern vases make an intriguing contrast with a marble fireplace, while the flowers' stunning dark shade provides a link.*
Right: *Dried lavender stuffed into vase-shaped baskets and a circle of seed heads and flowers provide scent and colour.*

if you live in a city and feel starved of the sight of greenery. Different types of flowers call up different atmospheres: overblown roses in an old cracked jug are reminiscent of the countryside in summer, while a structured arrangement of exotics may evoke the rigours of a glasshouse. The sight of tulips in a glass jar, bending and twisting as the days go by, can be as stimulating as any piece of sculpture. Foliage should not be forgotten: flowers look less formal when they have their own leaves with them, and an arrangement of ▶

fresh or dried leaves can be as attractive as any amount of colourful blooms.

The influence of the formal approach to arranging flowers is waning, overtaken by a preference for informality and simplicity. A single branch of cherry blossom or a careless handful of buttercups or cottage-garden blooms is gaining popularity over the tight pyramid of flowers carefully chosen for their regular appearance and particular colour. Fashions in flower arranging come and go so it is best to follow your own instinct for what you like, whether it be wild asymmetry, single blooms in separate vases, or a vase full of grasses without a flower in sight.

Flowers and foliage reflect the seasons. Daffodils are a sign of approaching spring, chrysanthemums signal the arrival of autumn. Winter is a wonderful time for foliage and berries, especially festive wreaths of yew and holly, and brightly coloured poinsettia.

A great variety of vegetation can be used successfully to decorate a house. Fat bunches of dried flowers or twigs are useful when the variety of fresh material is limited. Sheafs of ripened wheat or lavender stalks in urns make a change from roses in summer, and trees in pots bring the garden into the house. Box, bay and daisy trees can all be brought indoors and should be kept in shape to give a sophisticated look. Ivy tendrils are ideal for trailing across the mantelpiece, across the top of pictures and pelmets (cornices), twining between banisters or up candlesticks. If your supply of ivy is limited, it will be best used in quantity in a few places rather than spread around thinly and wispily.

Houseplants of any sort need attention to keep them in peak condition – not just watering but feeding, the right amount of light and heat and, some people claim, music and conversation. The danger with houseplants is that they can make a place look like a student hideout if they are not thoughtfully positioned.

Right top: *Thyme, rue, mint and other plants, all in blue pots against grey and white surroundings, thrive in the bathroom's steamy atmosphere and make a verdant setting for polished brass taps.*

Right bottom: *Richly-coloured autumn leaves and berries spill into bowls and on to the mantelpiece, at the same time picking out reds and yellows on china and teddy bear displayed alongside.*

Left: *Bare twisted branches in a vase on the floor are exactly in tune with the pale and elegant simplicity of the room's restrained decorations – a stunning contrast to the crowded fruitfulness opposite.*

Their effect on a room will depend on what they are and how many there are of them. Groups of plants can give a lusher, more abundant feel than isolated ones, although magnificent specimens can stand on their own. Ferns, for instance, can transform a bathroom into a romantic grotto.

In houses with sash windows, window boxes are an ideal playground for green fingers besides being refreshing and elegant in appearance. The contents can be changed each season to provide constant colour and variety. Bulbs can be planted for spring, annuals inserted in summer and replaced with winter-flowering pansies and ivy for the cold months. Herbs can be grown in window boxes as well as indoors in pots. The variety of colour and texture in their foliage is a pleasure for the eye to dwell on and their flavours will enliven food. With a little skill they can be made to last through the winter, long after herbs in the garden will have been overcome by frosts and harsh weather.

Artificial flowers can be decorative too. Some handpainted silk irises and lilies are the work of craftsmen who exactly capture their markings and subtle variations in colour. Artificial flowers are useful for augmenting natural ones and can even take their place, but there is nothing quite like the real thing.

POT-POURRI AND POMANDERS
The art of making sweet-smelling preparations from flowers, fruit and spices has been practised for centuries. The Elizabethans, for instance, were fond of carrying pomanders – small round perforated containers with refreshing scented matter inside – to ward off bad smells. Today the word 'pomander' is generally used to refer to a clove-studded orange. These are easy to make, give a delicious scent and have the added advantage of acting as a moth repellant. Pot-pourri's scented combination of essential oils and decorative dried flower petals, leaves and heads is still popular and made to many different recipes. You can choose a pot-pourri that will evoke the fragrant tropics or a rainy summer's day in the lush English countryside, or you can make your own.

KITCHENS

'The kitchen work was done communally both on the table, and on counters round the walls. And there might have been a comfortable old chair in the corner where someone could sleep through the activities.'

A Pattern Language 1977

Left: *Tongue-and-groove unit doors have been painted with a silky finish. The large porcelain butler's sink is the centre of activity and attention, accented by the glass-fronted cupboards above. Knives hanging on a magnet and glass storage jars add interest.*
Right: *Victorian tiles provide a bright and busy splashback for a marble sink and brass taps.*

The kitchen is the engine room of a home. Every room should be arranged according to its purpose, but in a kitchen an efficient layout is of paramount importance. Even if it is a large room for living in, its first priority is to work well. Unless you are lucky enough to have a scullery or laundry room, the household's machinery will be found here. With clever planning the kitchen can hold not only the food-related essentials like the stove and fridge, but all the other machines that lighten the burdens of domestic responsibility – the freezer, dishwasher, washing machine and dryer. By the finishing touches stage all such large equipment will be in place, and the challenge is to transform a utilitarian domestic office into a room in which it is a pleasure to cook or eat or just sit.

A streamlined 'designer' kitchen with everything matching can be fresh, elegant, easy to keep clean, and may be a great advantage in a small space. But large financial outlay is not the only route to a functional kitchen of character. A kitchen that has grown ▶

together piecemeal or where there are no fitted units other than the sink can be equally appealing, but probably a combination of the two extremes offers the best practical solution. It is important to bear in mind, however, that like any other room, the kitchen must be considered as a whole, including floor, ceiling and everything in between.

Most manufacturers of domestic machinery make what are called 'decor panel kits'. A kit is simply a new set of edges for the front of the machine in which there is space for a 'decor panel' to be inserted, to conceal the white enamel door. The panel can either be provided by the makers of the kitchen units, in which case the front of the machine will be almost indistinguishable from a cupboard unit, or it can be made from a piece of wood or other appropriate material and decorated in whatever way you wish. In a kitchen that is not streamlined in appearance this is an opportunity to be creative by making a collage of photographs, painting a piece of *trompe l'œil*, or reproducing an imaginary or real coat of arms. The same idea can be applied to all the cupboard doors in a kitchen.

The simplest way of drawing a less-than-beautiful piece of machinery into a kitchen's decorative scheme is with colour. Paint it the same colour as the walls or furniture, with either a brush or a spray. Washable eggshell (semi-gloss) or gloss paint is usually sufficiently hard-wearing, especially if a tough

Above: *Plates make ideal wall-decoration for kitchens since they can be easily wiped clean. The shapes and delicate tones of plain white and cream china can be as interesting as any amount of colour and pattern.*

Opposite: *The austerity of a charmingly old-fashioned kitchen is enlivened by paintings of fruit and other food, by the checked pattern of pale and dark floor tiles, and by sky-blue painted chairs and details.*

varnish or enamel is painted on to the handle and area around it, where the wear is heaviest. The same idea can be applied to any kitchen furniture and unit, and more than one colour can of course be used in the decorative scheme. Red, white and black; yellow and blue; terracotta and cream; or contrasting shades of the same colour – any combination applied with consistency will give the room the appearance of being a single entity rather than a furniture depot. The colour need not be applied flat; details can be picked out and patterns or special effects like marbling can be added. An alternative is to have a pure sparkling white kitchen enlivened by a display of china and objects in bright primary colours.

Scrubbed wooden chairs and cupboards, which may not have been designed as kitchen furniture, can pull a room together by virtue of the consistency of their material. Wooden

furniture that has ended up in the kitchen because it is in less-than-perfect condition, and furniture in different coloured woods, can be painted with coloured stain of the type that veils the wood but allows the grain to show through. The same colour should be used for all the furniture so that it looks as if it belongs together. Wooden knobs for cupboard doors can be stained in the same way, and another way of linking cupboards is by giving them knobs of a consistent type and colour.

A successful kitchen is one in which a virtue is made of practical necessity. The kitchen is primarily a place for preparing meals, and if the room is large enough, for eating them. It is obviously important that certain ingredients, implements and crockery are immediately to hand, and that others are stored in an organized way. Practical and decorative values need to be reconciled. Visually, it works to group similar articles together, to display those things that are varied and attractive to look at and to conceal those that are not, but the practical function of each object should also be considered. A dreary kitchen is one in which everything is hidden behind doors, revealing nothing of its owner's personality.

Knives can be stored in a wooden block or in order of size on a magnetic bar attached to the wall. Wooden spoons, spatulas and other similar implements can stand upright at one side of the stove (ideally on the right if you are right-handed) in a stone jar or a vase. Traditional kitchen-ware like old-fashioned enamel bread bins and earthenware bread crocks are attractive in an appropriate setting, and are useful for storing things other than bread if you prefer to keep bread in the fridge. Implements and small pans can be hung from a wooden or metal rack suspended with chains from the ceiling if it is sufficiently high. Vessels of identical material, such as pans made from copper, stainless steel or coloured enamel, are impressive when hung in order of size in a row on the wall or lined up together on a shelf. Collections of one type of glass or china can be arranged on a shelf or dresser — a collection of teapots, for instance, or decorative plates, or dishes of different designs but similar colour. (For suggestions about display see page 89.) Articles to keep out of sight include counter-top machines that are not used every day — these can be stored in a deep drawer for easy access.

Food is the *raison d'être* of the kitchen so it is appropriate to use its decorative possibilities to the full. Fresh fruit and colourful hard

vegetables like red-skinned onions can be stored in view in bowls or baskets. Some people prefer to keep their eggs out of the fridge, on a rack. Spices and herbs stored in visible rows of small glass or china jars are easier to get at when cooking than they are if jumbled together at the back of a cupboard. Larger storage jars are useful and can be decorative, especially glass ones that allow you to see when stocks are running low. The types of pasta, rice, dried beans and pulses that are used regularly should be placed within easy reach, but those used less frequently can be ranged in jars across the top of cupboards or wall units. Teas, coffees and tisanes should be stored in attractive airtight containers.

Every kitchen should have a cupboard or shelf for bottles. Plain and flavoured vinegars and nut and vegetable oils of various sorts are essential to imaginative cooking. A bottle of table wine should be kept within reach for casseroles and sauces, and perhaps some dry sherry as well. Some of these bottles will be clear glass, some brown and some green. The different colours and the variety of shapes and labels can make a group or row of bottles into an interesting still life. Two other ways of storing them within reach are to stack them in a small wine rack (first ensuring they have sound stoppers and will not leak) or to keep them in a square open-topped picnic basket

with divisions designed to receive bottles. They obviously cannot be seen so well stored in this way, but are easy to move about the kitchen as and when they are required.

Baskets of all kinds are useful and attractive in a kitchen. Available in a vast range of shapes and sizes, they provide easily transportable, self-contained storage space and can be hung from a rack or rail, or from the ceiling if it is the right height.

Wall space too can provide storage in the form of narrow shelves or a hanging rack. A half-height or full-height bookcase is a simple answer to storage problems and can look decorative if well organized. Pans and dishes can be arranged on its shelves, vegetables can be kept there in baskets or wire trays, storage jars can be lined up in rows and it is the obvious place for cookery books.

The walls of a kitchen can be decorated like those of any other room with framed pictures. For the sake of hygiene the frames should be simple and easy to wipe clean rather than gilded and ornate, and though the most appropriate subjects are ones relating to food that should not be a constraint. Since the kitchen is the most technical room in a home and in that sense necessarily modern, it is appropriate to hang contemporary pictures and posters there, especially if the decorations in the rest of the house are traditional.

Opposite: *This large kitchen is as much a room for living in as for cooking and eating, though these are its primary functions. Wicker baskets, polished wooden furniture and units contrast with plain white walls. Plates and pictures provide decoration and a stable door completes the farmhouse feel.*

Left: *With colour providing the unifying theme, a miscellany of household china can be as appealing as exactly-matching sets. Bowls, mugs, cups, jugs and plates are ranged on shelves and racks and even on the work surface, with hand-printed tiles and green-painted woodwork providing a fresh and interesting background.*

Below: *Open-fronted storage allows pans and dishes to be easily seen and retrieved. Regularly used, small stainless steel utensils are both attractive and handy when hung on butcher's hooks from a metal bar near the hob. Baskets provide portable storage for wooden spoons and other cutlery.*

BEDROOMS

'It is a sitting room, a place for privacy, a place for projects; the bed is part of it.'

A Pattern Language 1977

Left: *The bed is a bedroom's centre-piece, and the more striking it is the better. Furniture and pictures are grouped in deference to this magnificent iron and brass example.*
Right: *A large picture hung over the bed gives it importance. Upholstered headboards are ideal for sitting up against and reading in bed.*

The bedroom is a home's inner sanctum, a place for sleeping and dreaming and for coming to terms with the day ahead when you wake in the morning. In general it is the room in which you store your clothes and where you dress. It is the room in the house that is least likely to be seen by outsiders. For these reasons, it is quite usual for a bedroom to be decorated in a gentler style than the more public rooms. A living room or kitchen may be painted an invigorating shade of emerald green or lacquer red but a bedroom decorated in one of these colours is less restful than one predominantly sky-blue, sunny yellow or a deep soft green. In addition the bedroom is, inevitably, associated with romance, an impression to which the finishing touches can contribute significantly.

Male and female ideas of what constitutes romance vary as much in decorating terms as they no doubt do in real life, and at their worst extremes they are pure kitsch. There is the ultra-feminine nightmare in pink floral frills and flounces and its opposite ▶

number, the supposedly seductive combination of black satin sheets and low lighting.

True elegance is more likely to be found in romantic bedrooms decorated in the troubadour and old English styles. The troubadour style incorporates velvet and raw silk, Gothic patterns and dark polished wood. The lamps are of brass, gilded stucco or turned wood, there are richly patterned rugs on the floor and books by the bed are historical novels, thrillers and spy stories. The essence of the old English style is moss roses, white linen and the discreet use of lace – the most delicate and seductive of materials. Lamps are made from glass or adapted from Chinese vases, privacy is maintained by veils of spotted voile at the window, and books are romantic classics by Charlotte Brontë.

There are of course a hundred styles effective in a bedroom, ranging from Scottish baronial to post-modern. Interpretation of a single style varies hugely – Art Deco can mean round mirrors and languid curving lines, or it can be boldly black and white, with geometric lines and polished surfaces. As with the bathroom, the key to creating a bedroom is to think of the room as a whole entity with an independent character, not as a utilitarian space with no right to a distinctive personality.

The bed itself is the most significant element. It is the largest piece of furniture and the focus of attention, with other furniture arranged in deference to it. For the room to have character, the bed must have a sense of importance. Of all beds the divan is the blandest, but it can be rescued from insignificance by a magnificent headboard or coronet. A headboard can be made from anything from carved, turned or painted wood to upholstered chipboard (particle board). If you like to sit in bed reading or you enjoy breakfast in bed it is important to have a comfortable headboard – a carved oak panel would not be ideal. An upholstered headboard is extremely

Right top: Creamy walls and fabrics contrast with dark polished furniture and floor to create an impression of richness and restraint in this soothing and restful bedroom. Pictures add height to the bed.

Right bottom: Bottle green and ruby red make a dark, enveloping and essentially masculine bedroom. A mirror and pure white bed linen add highlights which prevent the room being gloomy.

comfortable, can be any shape and will provide a link between window curtains and the rest of the room if covered in the same fabric. Ideally the cover should be removable and the fabric washable. Arranging a bed so that a window is at its head can look effective, practical considerations apart.

A traditional way of giving a bed an air of magnificence and drama is to surmount it with a coronet. This is a semi-circular shelf, usually quite small and placed on the wall well above the head of the bed, from which curtains are hung. These can cover the wall and also be draped at each side of the bed. The shelf itself can be decorated with a pelmet (cornice) or valance or augmented with, for instance, a brass rail from which the curtains hang on rings. A bed placed side-on to the wall will look imposing and luxurious with a coronet placed above the middle of it, with the curtains hanging against the wall and around the head and foot. The coronet aims to create a similar effect to that given by a round half-tester, the difference being that the latter is an integral part of the bed.

Half-tester beds were also known as 'royal' beds in the early nineteenth century, an appropriate nickname since a half-tester makes a bed look like a throne. This type of bed is something like a four-poster without footposts. It has a canopy above it that is supported by the bed head (and sometimes from the ceiling as well) which extends over the upper half of the bed or along its entire length. The smaller half-testers are lighter in appearance and take up less room than four-posters, but are none the less grand. They can be semi-circular or square, wooden, metal or brass, and may be treated very simply or glorified with castellated fabric valances and heavy curtains. A dark, wooden half-tester bed can be hung with contrastingly pale, ethereal muslin, whereas a painted metal bed with shiny brass flourishes will look majestic

Left top: *A clothes rail or hand basin can be hidden behind a folding screen. Here, the screen and a pile of exotic cushions on the bed give dashes of rich colour to a pale and light room.*

Left: *Fabric with a large botanical design looks handsome on curtains and a tall upholstered bedhead, to which a display of plates draws extra attention. Personal photographs are at home in a bedroom.*

clothed in stiff raw silk and chintz material.

A large bedroom with sufficient space in it for a four-poster may also have room for a comfortable chair or small sofa. This will transform a merely functional room into a place with a life of its own. You can sit here and enjoy peace and quiet when other members of the household are entertaining or being rumbustious elsewhere. For the same reason, a bookcase or table where you can keep a collection of favourite and current volumes is a bonus. This is also true for a spare bedroom, where the selection should include books and brochures about local events, museums, art galleries, walks and other attractions to divert guests who stay with you.

The dressing table is a useful and necessary piece of bedroom furniture. It is also the second point of focus in the room after the bed, especially if the objects on it are chosen and arranged with thought. The first requirement is a mirror, either hung on the wall or, which is usually more practical, on a stand on the dressing table. This type of mirror can be swivelled to the best angle for the person sitting or standing in front of it. Some form of lighting, either natural or electric (essential for use after dark) or both, is important. Other objects on the dressing table depend entirely upon the taste and habits of its owner, but

Above left: The four-poster is still most people's idea of the ultimate romantic bed. White hangings, which ideally should be made from washable material, bring lightness to a solid structure.

Above right: Cool colours and fresh patterns create space in a small bedroom. Blue-and-white checks and stripes are unsophisticated, but have been cleverly mixed on bedcover and valance.

Opposite: Uncluttered and airy, this is a bedroom for the tidy-minded. The bed is positioned unconventionally, at an angle to the walls, to give the best possible view out of the curtainless window.

small enamel, silver and glass articles (such as boxes, bowls and a ring stand) look pretty upon a woman's dressing table. A man's dressing table can often be distinguished by silver-backed hair brushes and a bowl or tray for loose coins and all the other bits and pieces discarded from pockets at the end of the day. A bedroom is often the place favoured for displaying a collection of family photographs, perhaps in leather and silver frames of various sizes, on a table.

Bedside tables are invaluable homes for a lamp, glass of water, telephone and reading matter and, if placed each side of the bed, they need not be an identical pair. Any small piece of furniture such as a chest of drawers, chamber pot cupboard, whatnot or individual table of the right height can be commandeered as a bedside table. They should not be placed right up against the bed, in case you knock the contents on to the floor by accident in your sleep.

Bedroom clutter tends to consist of dirty laundry, spare blankets and empty suitcases. The first of these should be hidden in a receptacle of sufficient size to pre-empt the danger of overflow and made of material that blends in with its surroundings. Blankets need not be stored out of sight. If their colours are appropriate to the room's decorations they, and any spare eiderdowns and rugs, can be folded neatly and stacked on top of a low wardrobe. Old leather suitcases, which have an echo of the faded past, can be ruggedly attractive, but almost every other type of suitcase is better kept out of sight. (Ugly blankets can be stored in them with moth balls.) Hat boxes covered with patterned paper or painted an attractive colour provide decorative storage for small articles, including, of course, any hats that you may possess.

BATHROOMS

'Although your choice of basic fitments, wall and floor coverings set the style of your bathroom, it is the accessories that can make or mar the effect.'

Terence Conran
The Bed and Bath Book 1978

The bathroom is primarily a place for ablutions, but it also serves an important function as a room in which it is possible to relax totally. In a busy household it may be the only room in which you can close the door and forbid entry as a matter of course. The recipe of peace, quiet and a long hot soak is a powerful antidote to stress and weariness. An ideal bathroom provides the practical requirement of an efficient water supply in surroundings that are a pleasure to contemplate when wallowing in the bath.

The bath itself and other china fixtures will have been installed before the finishing touches stage, but it is nonetheless possible to affect radically the appearance of a bathroom with attention to detail. Are the taps (faucets) appropriate, for example? If not, they can be changed. If the bath is boxed in, the boxing can be decorated with polished panelling, painted beading, a special paint finish such as marbling, or a small mural of a watery subject like the nautical god Neptune, swimming fish or a seaside scene. ▶

Left: *A clinical composition in steel, tiling, mirror and wood, is created by broken reflections of the bath island and cylindrical hand basin in a wall of mirror-fronted cupboards. The polished floor gives warmth to this high-tech interior.*
Right: *Shells and dried plants add visual interest to a pale-coloured rustic tongue-and-groove bath surround.*

If you choose a mural it could be continued on the wall alongside the bath and the theme carried on around the room.

The areas of wall around the bath and above the hand basin are usually covered with tiling or glass panels as a protection against water that is inevitably splashed on them. Simple, mass-manufactured tiles can be made more interesting by being placed on the wall at a 45° angle, rather than at a right angle, to the bath, so that the lines between them make a diagonal trellis pattern rather than squares like graph paper. The bottom row can then be made up of triangular tiles in the same or a contrasting colour. Hand-made tiles from places such as Italy and Portugal offer a tantalizing choice of colours and designs. If tiling is continued up to the ceiling, it has a luxurious appearance and is advisable when there is a shower in the bath. Borders and contrasts of colour can be continued through the tiling – a black-and-white chequered line at waist, shoulder or ceiling height in a simple black and white bathroom, for example. Conversely, a tiled border need not stop where the general tiling ends but can continue across painted or papered walls.

Plain frosted glass is a reliable way of maintaining privacy at the bathroom window. It would be more original, however, to install

Square tiles can be set as diamonds, rectangular ones staggered like brickwork.

engraved, painted or stained glass, providing that it admits sufficient light. You could commission a glass panel the decoration of which continued the room's colours or incorporated your initials or other motifs. Another possible solution for a bathroom window is to hang coloured voile or patterned net across it, either flat or gathered. Since the bathroom is usually the smallest room in the house, and the dampest, it is not a place that lends itself to grand schemes with billowing fabric. Window curtains should be made of a fabric that can be washed. Blinds are an obvious alternative to curtains, because they take up less room and are more practical, and a blind can also be decorated in keeping with the room.

There are two lines of approach to decorating a bathroom – either to make a virtue of its small size or to challenge it. Making a virtue of it means using strong colours; challenging it involves creating an illusion of space with gentler colour and the generous use of mirror (of the type specially finished at the back to resist the effects of humidity). In both cases, lighting is important. Natural light should be made the most of and, if there is none (many apartments converted from houses have internal bathrooms), electric light needs to be well planned. There should be both general light over the whole room, and directed light

around the mirror used for greater accuracy when shaving, applying make-up or brushing teeth. This light need not be the regular and uninspiring mini-strip complete with shaver socket. The socket (if wanted) can be installed separately alongside the basin and the light can come from recessed or external spotlights or from wall-mounted bracket lights. Rows of bulbs in a panel up each side of the mirror can look good (and provide excellent light) in a bathroom with appropriately simple, modern decorations.

For a built-in, wall-to-wall mirror, lightweight mirror sheeting is ideal. It can be bought cut to size and simply glued on to the wall, although some other form of additional support is advisable, such as a batten placed under the bottom edge. A sheet mirror can be as large as you wish, so long as the piece can

Above: Tongue-and-groove boarding can be used to hide pipes and the lavatory cistern, at the same time providing a useful shelf. A mosaic floor is luxurious and practical, and blue is an apt colour for a bathroom.

Opposite top left: Plain reinforced glass screwed to the wall around the bath allows the walls' rag-rolled finish to show through; the radiator is ragged to disappear. The wooden bath rack holds sponge and pumice.

Opposite top right: Fashion prints with black-and-gold mounts link pale walls with black tiling around a bath with a view through an uncluttered window. Coloured towels dry on a heated rail.

be manoeuvred into the room for installation. It is worth giving some thought to what it will reflect. Some people find that too much of their own reflection can be disconcerting. Expanses of mirror placed on opposite walls will create an impression of an endless corridor as they reflect into one another. The effect is unsettling and generally to be avoided except perhaps in an intentionally bizarre or surreal scheme of decoration.

Any mirror, of any shape and size, will help enlarge a bathroom. The frame can be wooden – carved and gilded, perhaps, or of plain polished oak or bird's eye maple. Ordinary wooden framing can be decorated with geometric patterns, pictures and initials applied in oil paint or coloured enamel paint. Cut-outs and transfers of classical columns and architectural motifs can be stuck to a

Left: *A bold mixture of black-and-white patterns on floor, walls and shower curtain makes this a busy bathroom, but expanses of plain white tiling and the absence of other colours prevent the overall effect from being overwhelming.*

Right: *Carefully-positioned chequered and black borders add zest to an otherwise all-white bathroom. Bare light bulbs and daylight reflecting on the mirror and tiled floor make this a startlingly bright room for ablutions.*

and leaves. Modern spongeware soap dishes are decorated with a variety of flowers and animals. In choosing the design and colour of a soap dish, and of every other accessory in a bathroom, the style and colour scheme of the room should be borne in mind as it would in any other room, to avoid collecting a jumbled assortment of items with no visual consistency. Care must also be taken in choosing laundry baskets and other necessary articles like weighing scales. Unless their appearance is going to make a positive contribution to the room, they should be either concealed or banished altogether.

Visual impact will also be destroyed by a regiment of half-empty bottles of shampoo, bubble bath and all the other paraphernalia of modern grooming that accumulate in a bathroom, including the half-squeezed tube of toothpaste. Very few of these articles come in attractively designed vessels that are a pleasure to look at. Some of them, bubble bath for instance, can be transferred into glass jars and bottles which will make a colourful display at the end of the bath, on a shelf or on a window sill. The rest must be hidden in cupboards or stored discreetly in baskets.

Towels, on the other hand, make a strong visual contribution. Their colour can make or mar a bathroom and it is better to have plain white or cream if exactly the right colour cannot be found. Small hand towels are useful and can be exceptionally pretty and decorative, especially self-patterned linen, embroidered and appliquéd hand towels, and those with a straight or zigzagged border of lace or crochet. Towels in use must necessarily be on view while they air or dry, ideally on a heated towel rail or vertical radiator. If neither is possible, a towel rack placed over or in front of a radiator, or a folding frame like a clothes horse, are good alternatives.

plain frame and varnished. Any frame decorated in a watery or seaside theme is particularly appropriate. Shells, for example, can quite easily be applied to a mirror frame by covering it with plaster and pressing the shells into it while the plaster is still damp.

Mirrors can be successfully attached to the front of bathroom cupboards, providing camouflage as well as reflection. Circular shaving mirrors are useful, especially when attached to a concertina arm so that they can be folded away when not in use. For the man who likes shaving in the bath, the most luxurious mirror is one that stands up from a bath rack and is double sided – with normal and magnified reflection.

Bath racks are a source of contention. Some people find them a nuisance, others would not be without them. Certainly they are

one way of having soap and sponge at hand if there is no surface alongside the bath on which to put them and no soap dish attached to or recessed into the wall. Wooden, brass and chrome racks are the most handsome. Some small ones hang over the edge of the bath rather than being balanced across it, and small standing racks are made for a single bar of soap by the hand basin. These are a variation on the old-fashioned soap dish, an invaluable and decorative china contraption that helps keep soap dry between uses. It usually consists of three parts: a bowl underneath, a lid on top, and in between the drainer.

Old soap dishes are usually white on the inside and decorated on the outside. Twentieth-century ones generally have an overall colour and nineteenth-century ones are decorated with transfers and handpainted flowers

STAIRCASES

'A staircase is not just a way of getting from one floor to another. The stair is itself a space, a volume, a part of the building; and unless this space is made to live, it will be a dead spot.'

A Pattern Language 1977

The staircase is, in its own right, one of the most interesting elements in the house. Even when stripped of all colour and ornament, a staircase attracts the eye simply because of its structure. The zigzag of ascending steps, the smoothly rising handrail and the pattern of balusters which half screen the treads provide a rich variety of surfaces and angles. The most minimal modern staircase structure, in which the treads are cantilevered out of the wall without risers or balusters, is no less interesting than the most elaborate rococo confection and demands no less careful decorative treatment.

Almost every building retains its original staircase – unlike doors an 'unfashionable' staircase is, fortunately, not so cheaply or easily disposed of. The history of baluster shapes is fascinating, and the lively cut-out patterns of some seventeenth-century staircases particularly appealing. Until the nineteenth century, staircases in modest homes were generally made by joiners rather than specialists, and balusters were often plain ▶

Left: *A staircase can be treated as sculpture. Here, black-edged modern wooden cantilevered steps thrust sheer out of the white wall, leading the eye dramatically upwards. The figure of a man in a weight-lifting attitude beneath is a witty visual counterpoise.*
Right: *A slim iron spiral staircase fits neatly into a specially shaped passage end.*

wooden struts. Huge numbers of Victorian terrace houses have turned wooden balusters which were mass produced on lathes. If these have been painted repeatedly, the details of their form may be clogged as may the outlines of fret-cut brackets on the string – the panel running along the edge of the risers and treads – in grander houses. In this case restoration should be seriously considered, even if you plan to paint the wood again. It is, of course, possible to decorate in the style of the period of the house, but this may not be considered attractive today – woodwork in later Victorian houses was, for example, generally painted a dark colour such as black or brown. If you strip the wood, it will probably need feeding and polishing but beware, for the sake of safety, of making it too shiny and slippery. Staircases built of hardwoods such as oak should not be painted.

A painted staircase need not be one colour only. The most sophisticated *trompe l'œil* for a staircase is that which imitates a carpet stair runner. But any pattern suited to the type of

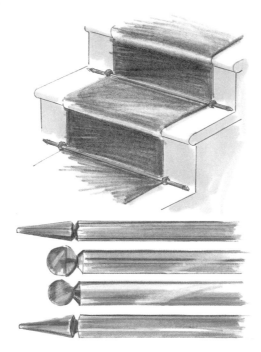

Brass stair rods are a handsome way of securing a runner or fitted stair carpet.

staircase can be painted on to it, or flat colour used to pick out structural detail. This method of decoration is particularly well suited to simple modern staircases. Balusters too can be decorated with paint, though there is a danger that turned wood balusters may look a trifle kitsch after this treatment. Cast- or wrought-iron balustrades should be painted black or white (or a deep blue or green), with subtle gold-leaf highlights if appropriate. Modern balusters, which may not be balusters at all in the traditional sense but a patterned geometric structure supporting the handrail, are the most receptive to painted colour.

STAIR CARPET

Carpet is a widely popular covering for stairs, either fitted or in the form of a woven runner. Until the nineteenth-century stair carpet was considered a luxury, and in households that were well-to-do but not wealthy it might be brought out only when there were visitors, bare polished wood sufficing for the rest of the time. Today, one of its great advantages is its effectiveness in reducing the noise of footsteps on the treads. In a busy household, or one where the inhabitants tend to run downstairs rather than walk, the noise on bare boards can be considerable.

On an old staircase built of softwood like pine the nosings of the treads are often worn or damaged and will need to be repaired or replaced, for safety, before carpet is laid over them. Fitted carpet that then continues along halls and passages can either be fitted right to the edge of the stairs or a little way in, leaving an area of polished or painted wood along each side. Carpet must fit tightly over each tread, either fixed in place with ready-made carpet grippers – wooden battens with numerous upstanding pins – or held in place by stair rods. Brass stair rods are cylindrical, flat or triangular; they frequently have decorative ends and are a fine sight when well polished.

Left: *Mellow terracottas, browns and yellows enrich the hall and staircase of an old house. Walls between beams have been removed leaving the bare structure, and tiles replace the stairs' worn-out treads.*

Opposite: *A staircase is sometimes the only place in a house with sufficient wall space for a large decorative hanging. Note also the hexagonal tiles on the floor and the sofa's simple and spacious loose cover.*

Opposite: *A simple staircase has been transformed by the treatment of the wood and adjoining wall with a variety of elaborate marbled paint finishes. The handrail is a coloured rope.*

Right: *The convention of vertical supports for the handrail has been abandoned in favour of a geometric pattern and large decorative panels which follow the angle of the staircase.*

Stairs need not be covered by runners designed for that purpose – narrow rugs such as kelims could be used in a sophisticated house and vibrantly coloured rag rugs in a cottage. Any carpeting will do so long as it is not slippery and is securely fixed in place. Rough matting made from coconut or sisal is a material that some decorators say one should use on stairs only with extreme caution because its surface can be slippery. Also for safety reasons, as well as convenience, the stairwell needs to be well lit.

HANDRAILS AND ROPES

Where the stairs rise up between two walls, as they frequently do in elderly cottages in which there would originally have been a simple wooden ladder, some sort of handrail should be provided in the interests of safety. A wooden rail, well polished for appearance and to prevent splinters, is a handsome traditional solution and extremely stable. (Solid mahogany rails can be rescued from architectural reclamation yards.) An alternative to this is a rope, either natural or coloured to tie in with the decoration of walls and stairs. Darker colours are more practical as lighter ones will tend to get dirty from handling. Thick coloured ropes are made especially for this purpose; they are supported by brass brackets fixed firmly to the wall and have a knot at each end to stop the rope slipping through. A rope hung from the top of the centre of a spiral staircase offers additional support in what can be a tricky structure to negotiate, especially at the narrow end of the treads.

DISPLAY

Spiral staircases and staircases that turn out of sight have a touch of mystery about them because you cannot see where they lead. Straight stairs also lead the eye upwards, usually to a landing or half-landing. Here, if there is sufficient space, it can be effective to put something as a focus of interest such as a table with objects upon it, a bold picture or an attractive arrangement of smaller pictures, a piece of sculpture or a large clock. If there is no room for furniture, a large mirror with an elaborate frame will serve the same purpose.

The wall that supports a staircase is bound to attract attention and can be used to display pictures of particular interest, which obviously need to be hung in steps that echo the stairs rather than in a straight horizontal line. Because this wall rises through two floors, offering a wall area perhaps larger than anywhere else in the house, it can provide a suitable space for a big painting or hanging. This should not be hung too low, for two reasons. Firstly, because it will be better seen across the width of a landing or where the stairs turn and, secondly, because a normal width of stair requires the person walking up the lower part to brush closer to the wall than would be the case in a room with furniture against or near the walls. This proximity of the viewer to displays on the staircase wall makes it a clever place to hang a collection of something that requires close examination, such as butterflies or fine engravings. A staircase should not be visually overburdened, however. It is already intrinsically interesting and unless it is consciously modelled on Dickens' old curiosity shop, complete with deep Victorian reds and greens, too many heavy frames and dark pictures hung on its walls may look confusing and oppressive.

INDEX

Numbers in italics refer to an illustration.

ACKNOWLEDGMENTS

The publisher would like to thank the following photographers and organizations for their kind permission to reproduce the photographs in this book:

8–9 Fritz von der Schulenburg (Monika Apponyi); 9 right Paul Ryan/J.B. Visual Press; 10 above Derry Moore; 10 below Jeremy Cockayne; 11 Ianthe Ruthven (Nicola Wingate-Saul, Print Rooms); 15 Guy Bouchet; 16 below right Fritz von der Schulenburg; 17 Richard Bryant/Arcaid; 18 Paul Ryan/J.B. Visual Press; 19 left J. Dirand/Stylograph; 19 right Jean-Pierre Godeaut (Designer: Lydia Kumel); 20 Jean-Paul Bonhommet; 21 Rodney Hyett/Elizabeth Whiting and Associates; 22 above Paul Ryan/J.B. Visual Press; 23 above Annet Held; 24–5 Richard Bryant/Arcaid; 26–7 Fritz von der Schulenburg (Richard Mudditt); 27 right Jean-Paul Bonhommet; 29 right Ianthe Ruthven (Charleston); 30 above Gilles de Chabaneix; 30 below Fritz von der Schulenburg (Barry Ferguson); 31 Paul Ryan/J.B. Visual Press; 32 Jean-Paul Bonhommet; 33 Jean-Pierre Godeaut; 34–5 Jean-Paul Bonhommet; 35 right Ianthe Ruthven; 37 right Jean-Paul Bonhommet; 39 left IPC Magazines/World Press Network; 40 Jean-Paul Bonhommet; 41 Paul Ryan/J.B. Visual Press; 43 right Derry Moore; 44 left Rodney Hyett/Elizabeth Whiting and Associates; 44 right Antoine Rozes; 45 Ianthe Ruthven (Hodgson House, Orford, New Hampshire); 47 right Derry Moore; 48 left Derry Moore; 48 right La Maison de Marie Claire (Maetaverne/Le Beau); 49 Fritz von der Schulenburg (Mimi O'Connell); 50–1 Ken Kirkwood (Lyn Le Grice); 52 left Vogue Living (Rodney Weidland); 52 right Mark Jones/Conran Octopus (Althea Wilson); 53 Camera Press; 54–5 David Phelps; 57 Jean-Paul Bonhommet; 58 Christian Sarramon; 59 Shona Wood/Conran Octopus (Polly Powell); 60–1 Derry Moore; 61 right Fritz von der Schulenburg (Christophe Gollut); 62 Gilles de Chabaneix; 65 Simon Brown/Conran

Octopus; 66–7 Richard Bryant/Arcaid; 67 right IPC Magazines/World Press Network; 69 IPC Magazines/World Press Network; 70 above Fritz von der Schulenburg (Karl Lagerfeld); 70 below Paul Ryan/J.B. Visual Press; 71 above Paul Ryan/J.B. Visual Press; 73 Gilles de Chabaneix; 75 right Jean-Paul Bonhommet; 76 Fritz von der Schulenburg (Suky Schellenberg); 77 Bent Rej; 78 Camera Press; 79 left Fritz von der Schulenburg (Bob Lawrence); 79 right Neil Lorimer/Elizabeth Whiting and Associates; 80 left Gilles de Chabaneix; 80 right Michael Crockett/Elizabeth Whiting and Associates; 81 Mike Nicholson/Elizabeth Whiting and Associates; 82–3 Richard Paul; 83 Guy Bouchet; 86 above Fritz von der Schulenburg (Janet Fitch); 86 below Jean-Paul Bonhommet; 87 below Jean-Paul Bonhommet; 88–9 Ken Kirkwood; 89 Paul Ryan/J.B. Visual Press; 90–1 Gilles de Chabaneix; 92 right Fritz von der Schulenburg; 93 left Karen Bussolini (Architect: Peter Kurt Woerner); 94 Pascal Chevalier/Agence Top; 95 left Jean-Paul Bonhommet; 95 right Derry Moore; 96 Richard Bryant/Arcaid; 97 Fritz von der Schulenburg (Andrew Wadsworth); 98–9 Jean-Pierre Godeaut; 99 right Linda Burgess/Conran Octopus; 100 Jacqui Hurst/Conran Octopus; 101 Roland Beaufre/Agence Top; 102–3 Fritz von der Schulenburg (Andrew Wadsworth); 103 right Paul Ryan/J.B. Visual Press; 104 left Gilles de Chabaneix; 104–5 Jean-Pierre Godeaut; 107 below Annet Held; 108–9 Lurdes Jansana/J.B. Visual Press; 109 right Derry Moore; 110 above Derry Moore; 110 below Andreas von Einsiedel/Elizabeth Whiting and Associates; 112 left Peter Woloszynski/Elizabeth Whiting and Associates; 113 Derry Moore; 115 right Houses & Interiors; 116 right Michael Dunne/Elizabeth Whiting and Associates; 118 Michael Dunne/Elizabeth Whiting and Associates; 119 Andreas von Einsiedel/Elizabeth Whiting and Associates;

120–1 Paul Ryan/J.B. Visual Press; 121 Richard Paul; 122 Camera Press; 123 Lars Hallen; 125 Boys Syndication.

The following photographs were specially taken for Homes & Gardens: 1–3 James Merrell; 4–5 Trevor Richards; 6–7 James Merrell; 7 right Christopher Drake; 12–13 James Merrell; 14 Tim Beddow; 16 above Les Mehan; 16 below left Tim Beddow; 22 below Clive Frost; 23 below Jan Baldwin; 28 James Merrell; 29 left James Merrell; 36 Tim Beddow; 37 left Christopher Drake; 38 Jan Baldwin; 39 right Jan Baldwin; 42 Trevor Richards; 43 left Jan Baldwin; 46 Jan Baldwin; 47 left Trevor Richards; 51 Christopher Drake; 56 James Merrell; 63 James Merrell; 64 Trevor Richards; 68 David Montgomery; 71 below Trevor Richards; 72 Jan Baldwin; 74–5 James Merrell; 84–5 Christopher Drake; 87 above James Merrell; 92 left Trevor Richards; 93 right Jan Baldwin; 100 right Linda Burgess; 106 Tim Beddow; 107 above James Merrell; 111 above James Merrell; 111 below David Montgomery; 112 right James Merrell; 114–5 Trevor Richards; 116 left Jan Baldwin; 117 Les Mehan; 124 James Merrell.

The author would like to thank: Katrin Cargill; Antony Beevor; Heather Hilliard.